The media's watching Vault!
Here's a sampling of our coverage.

"For those hoping to climb the ladder of success, [Vault's] insights are priceless."
– *Money magazine*

"The best place on the web to prepare for a job search."
– *Fortune*

"[Vault guides] make for excellent starting points for job hunters and should be purchased by academic libraries for their career sections [and] university career centers."
– *Library Journal*

"The granddaddy of worker sites."
– *US News and World Report*

"A killer app."
– *New York Times*

One of Forbes' 33 "Favorite Sites"
– *Forbes*

"To get the unvarnished scoop, check out Vault."
– *Smart Money Magazine*

"Vault has a wealth of information about major employers and job-searching strategies as well as comments from workers about their experiences at specific companies."
– *The Washington Post*

"A key reference for those who want to know what it takes to get hired by a law firm and what to expect once they get there."
– *New York Law Journal*

"Vault [provides] the skinny on working conditions at all kinds of companies from current and former employees."
– *USA Today*

Decrease your T/NJ Ratio
(Time to New Job)

Use the Internet's most targeted job search tools for finance professionals.

Vault Finance Job Board
The most comprehensive and convenient job board for finance professionals. Target your search by area of finance, function, and experience level, and find the job openings that you want. No surfing required.

VaultMatch Resume Database
Vault takes match-making to the next level: post your resume and customize your search by area of finance, experience and more. We'll match job listings with your interests and criteria and e-mail them directly to your inbox.

VAULT
> the most trusted name in career information™

FOR USE IN
OFFICE OF CAREER SERVICES
ONLY
If photocopies are desired
please ask Librarian for assistance.

VAULT GUIDE TO
THE TOP ACCOUNTING FIRMS

© 2004 Vault Inc.

Competition on the Street – and beyond – is heating up. With the finance job market tightening, you need to be your best.

We know the finance industry. And we've got experts that know the finance environment standing by to review your resume and give you the boost you need to snare the financial position you deserve.

Finance Resume Writing and Resume Reviews

- Have your resume reviewed by a practicing finance professional.
- For resume writing, start with an e-mailed history and 1- to 2-hour phone discussion. Our experts will write a first draft, and deliver a final draft after feedback and discussion.
- For resume reviews, get an in-depth, detailed critique and rewrite within TWO BUSINESS DAYS.

Finance Career Coaching

Have a pressing finance career situation you need Vault's expert advice with? We've got experts who can help.

- Trying to get into investment banking from business school or other careers?
- Switching from one finance sector to another – for example, from commercial banking to investment banking?
- Trying to figure out the cultural fit of the finance firm you should work for?

"Thank you, thank you, thank you! I would have never come up with these changes on my own!"
– W.B., Associate, Investment Banking, NY

"Having an experienced pair of eyes looking at the resume made more of a difference than I thought."
– R.T., Managing Director, SF

"I found the coaching so helpful I made three appointments!"
– S.B., Financial Planner, NY

For more information go to http://finance.vault.com

VAULT
> the most trusted name in career information™

VAULT GUIDE TO
THE TOP ACCOUNTING FIRMS

**DEREK LOOSVELT
AND THE STAFF OF VAULT**

© 2004 Vault Inc.

Copyright © 2004 by Vault Inc. All rights reserved.

All information in this book is subject to change without notice. Vault makes no claims as to
the accuracy and reliability of the information contained within and disclaims all warranties.
No part of this book may be reproduced or transmitted in any form or by any means,
electronic or mechanical, for any purpose, without the express written permission of Vault Inc.

Vault, the Vault logo, and "the most trusted name in career information™" are trademarks of
Vault Inc.

For information about permission to reproduce selections from this book, contact Vault Inc.,
150 West 22nd St, New York, New York 10011, (212) 366-4212.

Library of Congress CIP Data is available.

ISBN 1-58131-285-7

Printed in the United States of America

ACKNOWLEDGEMENTS

Vault would like to acknowledge the assistance and support of Matt Doull, Ahmad Al-Khaled, Lee Black, Eric Ober, Hollinger Ventures, Tekbanc, New York City Investment Fund, American Lawyer Media, Globix, Hoover's, Glenn Fischer, Mark Fernandez, Ravi Mhatre, Carter Weiss, Ken Cron, Ed Somekh, Isidore Mayrock, Zahi Khouri, Sana Sabbagh and other Vault investors. Many thanks to our loving families and friends.

This book could not have been written without the extraordinary efforts of Marcy Lerner, Laurie Pasiuk, Chris Prior and Elena Boldeskou. Thanks also to Mike Baker, Hussam Hamadeh, Samer Hamadeh, Keith Kirkpatrick, Danielle Koza, Todd Kuhlman, Mark Oldman, Kristy Sisko and Thomas Nutt.

Special thanks to all of the recruiting coordinators and corporate communications representatives who helped with the book. We appreciate your patience with our repeated requests and tight deadlines.

The *Vault Guide to the Top Accounting Firms* is dedicated to the accounting professionals who took time out of their busy schedules to be interviewed or complete our survey.

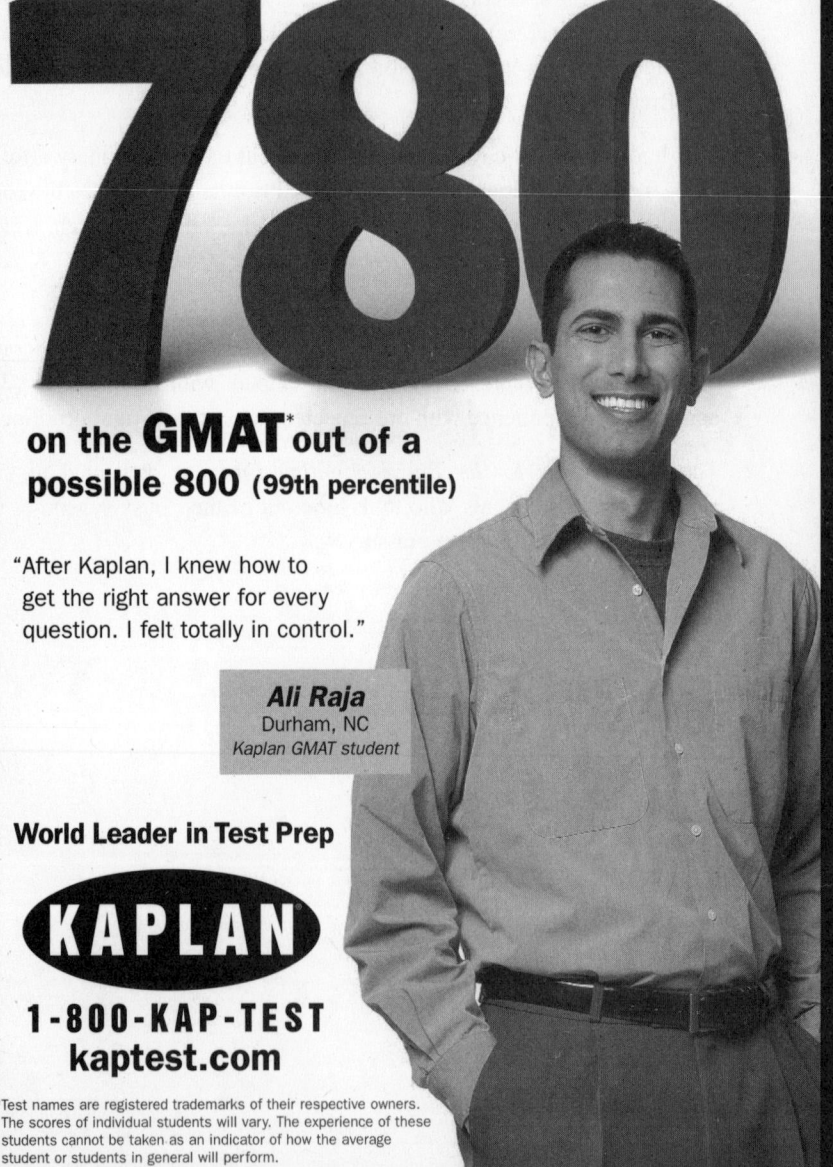

Table of Contents

INTRODUCTION 1

Introduction 3
A Guide to This Guide 12

TOP FIRM PROFILES 15

BDO Seidman LLP 16
BKD LLP 20
Clifton Gunderson LLP 24
Crowe Chizek and Company LLC 28
Deloitte & Touche LLP 32
Ernst & Young LLP 44
Grant Thornton LLP 54
KPMG LLP 62
McGladrey & Pullen LLP 72
Moss Adams LLP 76
Plante & Moran PLLC 80
PricewaterhouseCoopers LLP .84

THE BEST OF THE REST 93

Berdon LLP 94
Cherry, Bekaert & Holland LLC 95
Dixon Odom PLLC 96
Eide Bailly LLP 97
Eisner LLP 98
Goodman & Co. 99
J.H. Cohn LLP 100

LarsonAllen (Larson, Allen, Weishair & Co.) LLP 101
Parente Randolph LLC 102
Reznick Fedder & Silverman 103
Rothstein, Kass & Co. 104
Schenk Business Solutions 105
Virchow, Krause & Co. 106
Weiser LLP 107
Wipfli (Wipfli Ullrich Bertelson) LLP 108

APPENDIX 109

Accounting Glossary 111
About the Author 119

Decrease your T/NJ Ratio
(Time to New Job)

Use the Internet's most targeted job search tools for finance professionals.

Vault Finance Job Board
The most comprehensive and convenient job board for finance professionals. Target your search by area of finance, function, and experience level, and find the job openings that you want. No surfing required.

VaultMatch Resume Database
Vault takes match-making to the next level: post your resume and customize your search by area of finance, experience and more. We'll match job listings with your interests and criteria and e-mail them directly to your inbox.

VAULT CAREER GUIDES
GET THE INSIDE SCOOP ON TOP JOBS

"Cliffs Notes for Careers"
– FORBES MAGAZINE

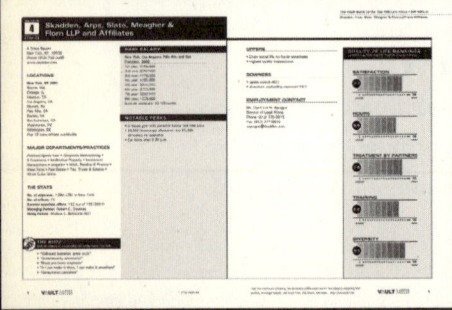

Vault guides and employer profiles have been published since 1997 and are the premier source of insider information on careers.

Each year, Vault surveys and interviews thousands of employees to give readers the inside scoop on industries and specific employers to help them get the jobs they want.

"To get the un-varnished scoop, check out Vault"
– SMARTMONEY MAGAZINE

VAULT

INTRODUCTION

Competition on the Street – and beyond – is heating up. With the finance job market tightening, you need to be your best.

We know the finance industry. And we've got experts that know the finance environment standing by to review your resume and give you the boost you need to snare the financial position you deserve.

Finance Resume Writing and Resume Reviews

- Have your resume reviewed by a practicing finance professional.
- For resume writing, start with an e-mailed history and 1- to 2-hour phone discussion. Our experts will write a first draft, and deliver a final draft after feedback and discussion.
- For resume reviews, get an in-depth, detailed critique and rewrite within TWO BUSINESS DAYS.

Finance Career Coaching

Have a pressing finance career situation you need Vault's expert advice with? We've got experts who can help.

- Trying to get into investment banking from business school or other careers?
- Switching from one finance sector to another – for example, from commercial banking to investment banking?
- Trying to figure out the cultural fit of the finance firm you should work for?

"Thank you, thank you, thank you! I would have never come up with these changes on my own!"
– W.B., Associate, Investment Banking, NY

"Having an experienced pair of eyes looking at the resume made more of a difference than I thought."
– R.T., Managing Director, SF

"I found the coaching so helpful I made three appointments!"
– S.B., Financial Planner, NY

For more information go to http://finance.vault.com

VAULT
> the most trusted name in career information™

Introduction

Accounting isn't just for rumpled men in green eyeshades anymore – and it hasn't been for some time. Accountants no longer pore over illegible balance sheets; nowadays, these professionals do their work on computers and advise their clients on the best way to handle their taxes and finances. It's more accurate, in fact, to call your average accountant a "financial services professional."

The accounting industry has been getting more than its share of scrutiny lately, ever since a series of ethical failures came to light beginning in 2001. These brought accounting into disrepute, and caused the SEC to take a hard look at the profession and its members. New legislation like the Sarbanes-Oxley Act has been introduced to prevent a failure of accounting standards in the industry, changing the structure of accounting and professional services firms in the process.

State of the industry

The accounting industry is dominated by a group of firms called the Big Four: Ernst & Young, PricewaterhouseCoopers, KPMG and Deloitte & Touche. Although these firms are massive and represent the status quo in the industry, they are quite a volatile bunch. In fact, the cream of the accounting field was known as the Big Eight prior to 1989, becoming the Big Six in the mid-1990s. In 1998, Price Waterhouse and Coopers & Lybrand merged to form the giant firm PricewaterhouseCoopers, making the Big Five. Ernst & Young and KPMG attempted a similar merger, only to quail at European regulatory concerns. The failure of Enron in 2002, a Fortune 100 company audited by Arthur Andersen, led to the prosecution of Andersen (the first-ever criminal prosecution of a corporation) and the subsequent dissolution of its accounting practice. Industry wits, possibly inspired by their annual college basketball office pools, have toyed with the designation "The Final Four" for the remaining big players.

Accounting firms enthusiastically grew their consulting units in the 1980s and 1990s. The Securities and Exchange Commission (SEC) is growing increasingly concerned that this presents a conflict of interest and has moved to regulate the consulting services accounting firms can offer clients that they audit. The Big Four have sought to spin off or sell accounting units; Andersen was forced to arrange the sale of Andersen Business Consulting to KPMG, a deal announced in May 2002. PwC announced plans to deal its consulting business, complete with 30,000 personnel, to IBM in July 2002; the $3.5 billion sale was completed in October 2002, with half of PwC's consultants laid off and the other half becoming part of IBM Business Consulting Services. Currently, only Deloitte offers management consulting as part of its primary service portfolio.

The Enron aftermath

One of the biggest news stories of 2002 was the bankruptcy of Enron, an energy trader accused of shoddy accounting practices. Besides shareholders and employees, the Enron scandal also took as its victim one of the most prominent firms in the accounting profession: Andersen, Enron's auditor. In May 2002, Arthur Andersen became a firm under siege: undergoing Justice Department prosecution for obstruction of justice, watching the resignation of its worldwide leader, suffering a constant stream of client defections, and losing staff and partners both domestically and worldwide. After divestiture talks with Ernst & Young, KPMG and Deloitte & Touche all faltered, the firm suffered the equivalent of the death penalty for an accounting corporation: in June 2002, it was legally barred from auditing public companies. The firm appealed, but the verdict was upheld in September 2002. This event has had a number of outcomes, including higher audit costs, increased SEC and client scrutiny of auditor performance, a flight of clients to lower-cost, second-tier accounting firms, and increased auditor independence as they become less beholden to consulting fees.

The unfortunate results of the Enron affair are dramatic and far-reaching: the largest bankruptcy in U.S. history, $32 billion lost in market capitalization, $1 billion lost in employee retirement accounts, and the first-ever felony indictment of a public accounting firm by the Justice Department. Furthermore, the scandal, along with other recent, high profile audit failures at companies such as Waste Management and Cendant, has damaged the integrity and credibility of the public accounting profession in the eyes of senior executives and the public at large.

The Sarbanes-Oxley Act

The most obvious legal upshot of the accounting scandals is the introduction of the Sarbanes-Oxley Act of 2002. This piece of legislation, enacted in June 2002, establishes a number of controls and prohibitions for firms engaged in accounting and auditing. These include the formation of a five-member Public Company Accounting Oversight Board (PCOAB), appointed by and answerable to the SEC; the prevention of accounting firms performing certain business consulting functions (note the sale of Andersen's and PwC's consulting practices); a requirement that individual audit partners must be rotated at least once every five years; and the establishment of criminal penalties for certain activities.

Sarbanes-Oxley has a number of provisions and exceptions, and would require a separate overview to explain in anything approaching full detail. Fortunately, there is no shortage of analysis and coverage of the new law; everybody from the government to CPA associations to business magazines has their own digest of the rules and their potential impact on the industry. Undergrad and grad students, especially accountants, will learn all about it in the slew of business ethics course that have become a larger part of b-school curricula.

Public accounting

Public accounting involves working for a service firm that provides, among other things, accounting and tax advisory services to a list of clients. These clients may be large corporations or regional businesses, governments, nonprofit organizations, or individuals. The public accounting industry typically is divided into three segments: the aforementioned Big Four, the regional firms, and the locals.

The Big Four is composed of the four largest public accounting firms in the world, each possessing an international client base and offering a very diverse group of services. These include PricewaterhouseCoopers, Ernst & Young, KPMG and Deloitte & Touche. This select group audits the vast majority of the Fortune 500. The marquee client base that these firms possess will be heavily touted during any marketing activities each firm undertakes, whether recruiting- or client development-oriented in nature.

The regional accounting firms are those that likely have some national service lines and possibly some international clients, but largely tend to have strong practices within the United States. In short, the largest regional firms can be thought of as somewhat smaller versions of Big Four firms. As their name suggests, these practices tend to be stronger in certain regional locations. If you are considering working for a regional public accounting firm, be sure to research the quality of the firm's practice in your particular area. The large regional players include Grant Thornton and BDO Seidman. Local accounting firms operate in a small number of cities and tend to be focused on small businesses and individuals. These organizations will likely conduct more tax and tax planning-driven engagements, and traditionally handle more of the bookkeeping responsibilities for their clients.

Most public accountants are CPAs: Certified Public Accountants. This certification provides an advantage in the job market because it is not easy to come by. To get a CPA certificate, accountants must pass a rigorous two-day, four-part exam. Only about one quarter of candidates pass all four parts each year, but most states only require candidates to pass two parts initially, and the other two within a certain period of time. Generally, applicants must also have a college degree and some accounting experience.

Industry accounting

When referring to industry accounting, people usually speak of working directly for an operating company as a staff accountant. The term "industry" is likely a result of the fact that public accountants tend to be generalists early in their career (rather than people who work for one company who can develop much more insight into the specific industry within which the company operates).

The potential job responsibilities for an industry accountant are quite broad and non-standardized as compared to public accounting. Many areas within a company have the need for professional accounting staff. These areas include: treasury and corporate finance, financial reporting, cost management, internal audit, performance evaluation, and business development. Such positions are offered at both a corporate and business unit level. The corporate level positions tend to offer more generalist skill-specific roles, versus the typically broader and more industry- or product-specific roles found within business units.

Accounting culture

One contact characterizes the accounting firm atmosphere as "pretty conservative," but doesn't seem to suffer from stuffiness. "For the tax and audit side, I can relate that individuals I have spoken with have reported that the culture seems to be one that is open, fun, hardworking and hard playing." Another agrees, adding that "the office environment is one of team spirit and camaraderie." The average workweek is around "50 to 55 hours during the busy season and less during the summer," one contact tells us. Another notes that "you might get screwed now and again and have to work long hours, but personally I have nothing at all to complain about."

Merry in the middle

Employees at smaller firms say there are many benefits of working for a middle market accounting firm. "We have the size, name and resources," says one source, "but you are not treated like just another number, which many of my friends in [Big Four] firms tell me they are." Another contact comments on the breadth of experience: "We are on a different project every three or four months. I have seen the resumes of people who have been doing this for three or four years and can honestly say they are qualified for upper-level management jobs at major corporations." One source explains that compared to larger firms, accountants at middle market firms have more autonomy, and the atmosphere in general is "much more laid-back."

Think outside the paycheck

Salaries for junior accountants, in the words of a contact, are in the range of "$30,000 to $40,000 starting plus overtime – nothing to spit on." Still, accountants at smaller firms feel that their work isn't the best paying. But if a firm that's grown steadily for the past three decades offers its employees shares, they'll be rewarded in other ways. "We're not known for paying the most in the marketplace, but it is fair and there is a lot more to a job than money," says one employee. Concludes another source, "There is a very noticeable focus on participation in the various stock purchase/stock option programs, which have proven to be very profitable for employees over the years." According to one insider, "What one quickly discovers is that salary represents only one form of compensation." Perks include matching 401(k) programs, laptop computers and palm pilots, clubroom membership at airline lounges, and many, many frequent flyer miles.

Troubles in the diversity department

Representation of minority groups doesn't seem to be one of the industry's strong suits. But one contact stresses that some offices do have an impressive international mix. "There are many international staff members throughout the firm. You are as likely to work with Russians, Chinese, Japanese and Muslims as you are to work with Anglo-Saxons." One West Coast accountant says, "We have a lot of different employees from all over the world here in L.A."

Firms have tried to promote gender diversity, and one source tells us that being a member of a minority group "would not affect your career in any way." However, another source has a different story: "I honestly would not want to be a woman in my practice – my group is very much male-dominated, and several of these men have problems taking women seriously. We've lost a few women recently because of this." The same contact qualifies this by observing that his firm's New York office has "several female managers."

Sartorial roller coaster

Though some insiders say their firms are slowly adopting a more casual dress policy, most indicate that dress is generally formal. "Suits are required year-round, except for Fridays and during the summer," reports one source. "Then it's business casual. However, if you go to a client, you wear what they wear." Another agrees, noting, "we have a strict dress code, but introduced two business casual months for the first time this year."

Training

Accounting starts off with intensive training for those lucky enough to be hired. A main differentiating factor between industry and public accounting is the volume and depth of training available to employees of large public accounting firms. Many of the Big Four and the larger regional firms have dedicated training centers with full-time educational staff and/or employ nationally renowned topical experts to conduct seminars for their personnel. Within the first year of a public accounting staffer's career, he or she can expect to receive approximately three weeks of formal educational training.

Summer internships

Most large public accounting firms utilize summer interns to varying degrees depending on the hiring practices in a particular region, as well as the current state of the employment market. The best advice on how to seek a summer internship for public accounting is to utilize a two-pronged approach. First, leverage the resources of your school. Many formal accounting education programs have existing relationships that can assist you in your search. Your accounting professors, professional clubs and departmental office personnel should all be viewed as potential networking opportunities. Additionally, those firms that actively recruit on your campus may offer intern positions as a chance to try out potential full-time hires. Second, pursue those organizations with which you are interested in full-time employment, even if they do not actively recruit at your school. The initial contact can lead to a greater chance of receiving a permanent placement interview, even if an internship selection does not result.

Summer internships are valuable in that they offer students a chance to view exactly what the first few years of job responsibilities will look like within a particular firm. Usually, summer interns are asked to perform similar duties to first-year full-time employees. Another possibility is to consider taking a semester off from classes to pursue an internship with a firm during its "busy season" – typically the period between January and April. This can result in credit towards an accounting degree as well as a large lead in climbing the experience curve. Many public accountants claim they learn more during this period than during any other time during the year. Stated one former senior accountant from the Big Five era, "Learning definitely comes in waves within this industry. Those particular three months represent a tidal wave of learning."

Audit

Formally known as an examination engagement under the standards of the AICPA (American Institute of Certified Public Accountants), this assignment culminates with a partner of the firm signing an audit opinion regarding a company's financial statements. In short, this means they agree that a set of financial statements is "fairly stated" (i.e., that the assets exist, the liabilities are real and complete, and the cash flows, income, and expense amounts are correct). Full audit procedures are utilized when issuing such an opinion. In recent years, the use of computers has drastically changed the audit process.

Statistical sampling programs, high-powered database programs, and "intelligent" audit computer programs (which walk an auditor through the exact steps to be performed utilizing a questionnaire format) now exist. This change does not totally eliminate the use of the paper trail during an audit, but does reduce the amount of documentation that is handwritten. Additionally, it helps the larger firms reduce their audit risks, as they can standardize their audit approaches using such programs.

Review

Designed by the AICPA to be less in its scope than a full financial statement audit, a review offers a limited statement of assurance on a set of financials and does not involve such extensive audit procedures. In practice, this usually involves a much more conversational auditing style during which auditors do not use as many sampling and vouching techniques. During the first few years of a public accountant's career, the role he or she assumes during a review is very similar to that for an audit.

Career path

Because public accounting is a mature industry, people entering with the idea of making a lifelong career of the profession should take note. The partnership tracks at the larger firms are continuing to lengthen and involve many more steps along the path than ever before. Many professionals have found that transferring to a specialty line within a large accounting firm has offered them increased opportunities for advancement when compared to the traditional audit and tax departments. Be sure that you understand the current requirements to make partner within any specific firm with which you accept a job. Also, know that due to these industry factors, it will likely be more difficult than you are actually told to reach such a position.

Traditionally, public accounting firms have held an "up-or-out" attitude in their retention practices. While recently this has changed slightly at the manager and partner levels, it still very much exists at the lower levels of these organizations. A public accounting firm employee needs to take an active role in monitoring and managing his career so that no news comes as a surprise. If an employee is let go – and it does happen more frequently than most firms speak of – he or she is usually given a grace period to search for a new job. In general, public accounting firms view ex-employees as potential clients and treat them professionally.

The traditional title groupings that most large accounting firms use are as follows:

Staff: Usually have one to three years of professional experience. The responsibilities include performance of detailed audit work and completion of many of the administrative tasks surrounding an audit.

Senior: Usually have two to five years of professional experience. Their main responsibilities include supervision of the staff performing the detailed audit work and reporting those results to the manager and partner assigned to the client. Additionally, the Senior usually handles much of the audit planning for engagements. In general, the primary "workhorse" of an audit is the senior. Many long-term ex-public accountants describe working more hours at this level of responsibility than any other.

Manager: The manager has overall responsibility for client planning and interaction. Managers are required to identify opportunities for partners to sell some work. They oversee engagements at a macro level, leaving the details to the senior to handle. The tenure at the manager level is entirely dependent on the firm and the individual's position within it. In general, it is a long career track to partnership. The first opportunity for promotion to partner is at a minimum about five years.

Partner: The main role of the partner is as a rainmaker, establishing and maintaining relationships with clients. Younger partners tend to be more sales-oriented.

Opportunity knocks

Even before Enron, the accounting profession witnessed a significant decrease in new membership. The number of students graduating with accounting degrees fell 23 percent from 1996 to 2000, as students turned increasingly to careers in finance, information technology, and other business disciplines. The taint from the Enron scandal could further deter students from pursuing an accounting career. However, the increased emphasis on the quality of accounting and auditing could make the profession more attractive to students seeking challenging, meaningful assignments and high levels of responsibility.

A Guide to This Guide

All of our profiles follow the same basic format. Here's a guide to each entry.

Firm facts

- **Departments:** The firm's major divisions.

- **The Stats:** Basic information about the firm, usually information that's available to the general public. This includes the firm's leadership (generally, the person responsible for day-to-day operations, though it can include the chairman and relevant department heads), employer type (e.g., public, private, or subsidiary), ticker symbol and exchange (if public), 2002 revenue and net income (usually only for public companies; we do have some estimates from third-party sources for private companies and in some cases, the firm has confirmed that information), number of employees and number of offices.

- **Key Competitors:** The firm's main business rivals. Size, business lines, geography and reputation are taken into account when evaluating rivals.

- **Uppers and Downers:** The best and worst things, respectively, about working at the firm. Uppers and downers are taken from the opinions of insiders based on our surveys and interviews.

- **Employment Contact:** The person (or people) that the firm identifies as its contact(s) for submitting resumes or employment inquiries. We've supplied as much information as possible, including names, titles, mailing addresses, phone or fax numbers, e-mail addresses and web sites. Because companies process resumes differently, the amount of information may vary. For example, some firms ask that all employment-related inquiries be sent to a central processing office, while other firms mandate that all job applications be submitted through the company web site.

The profiles

Most profiles are divided into three sections: The Scoop, Getting Hired and Our Survey Says; (some profiles have only Scoop and Getting Hired sections).

- **The Scoop:** The company's history, a description of the business, recent clients or deals and other significant developments.

- **Getting Hired:** An overview of the company's hiring process, including a description of campus recruiting procedures, the number of interviews, questions asked and other tips on getting hired.

- **Our Survey Says:** Quotes from surveys and interviews done with employees or recent employees at the company. Includes information on culture, pay, hours, training, diversity, offices, dress code and other important company insights.

Decrease your T/NJ Ratio
(Time to New Job)

Use the Internet's most targeted job search tools for finance professionals.

Vault Finance Job Board
The most comprehensive and convenient job board for finance professionals. Target your search by area of finance, function, and experience level, and find the job openings that you want. No surfing required.

VaultMatch Resume Database
Vault takes match-making to the next level: post your resume and customize your search by area of finance, experience and more. We'll match job listings with your interests and criteria and e-mail them directly to your inbox.

> the most trusted name in career information™

TOP FIRM PROFILES

BDO Seidman LLP

180 N. Stetson., Ste. 4300
Chicago, IL 60601
Phone: (312) 240-1236
Fax: (312) 240-3329
www.bdo.com

DEPARTMENTS
Assurance
Business Development
Consulting
Corporate Finance
Financial Advisory
Healthcare
Internal Audit/Risk Consulting
Litigation Support
Taxation (Domestic, International)
Real Estate
SEC

THE STATS
Chairman and Interim CEO: Jack Weisbaum
CEO: Denis Field (currently on a leave of absence)
Employer Type: Private partnership (member firm of BDO International)
Revenue: $353 million (FYE 6/02)
No of. Employees: 1,950
No. of Offices: 35

KEY COMPETITORS
Deloitte & Touche
Ernst & Young
KPMG
PricewaterhouseCoopers

UPPERS
- Big Four capability, small-firm feeling

DOWNERS
- Still not the Big Four

EMPLOYMENT CONTACT
130 E. Randolph, Ste. 2800
Chicago, IL 60601
Phone: 312-240-1236
Fax: 312-240-3311
www.bdo.com/careers

THE SCOOP

Number five

BDO Seidman is the U.S. arm of BDO International, the top firm in the so-called "second tier" of accounting firms worldwide, just below the Big Four. BDO International has nearly 600 offices in 100 countries, while the U.S. unit BDO Seidman has 35 offices and nearly 175 alliance firm locations throughout the country. Founded in 1910 as Seidman & Seidman, the firm was run by members of the Seidman family until the mid-1970s, when William Seidman left the firm to join the Ford Administration and ultimately to manage the FDIC. Today, BDO Seidman provides accounting and consulting services, including auditing, corporate finance, tax consulting, arbitration, and management consulting services. Headquartered in Chicago, Ill., the company has increasingly focused on tax strategy in the 1990s, but recent litigation filed by the IRS against the firm's aggressive tax consulting services have forced the company to modify its corporate plans.

A new focus

In 2002, the IRS began investigating the firm's use of tax-shelter fees to generate additional profits, and the IRS has requested the related documents. In an article in *The Wall Street Journal* on October 24, 2003, documents included in government court filings show CEO Denis Field urging partners in a 1999 presentation to "think green," stressing that a $1 million tax-shelter fee would generate as much profit as $5 million of hourly billings for conventional accounting work. Although the matter is still pending, BDO Seidman's chief has taken an indefinite leave of absence and five of the 12 members on the company's board have been replaced.

Nonetheless, the company maintains that these changes are unrelated to the pending IRS litigation, and are simply a step in refocusing the firm to account for overall changes occurring in the accounting field. Perhaps as an indication of the company's new focus, Reuters reported on October 9, 2003, that Kmart Holding Corp. announced it had dismissed PricewaterhouseCoopers as its independent auditor and appointed BDO Seidman in its place.

More trouble?

BDO Seidman isn't out of the woods of scandal. In a lawsuit that names BDO Seidman and a unit of American International Group for their alleged role in a tax shelter, Milan Mandaric, chairman of a well-known soccer team in the U.K., is suing various advisers for promoting a strategy that generated tax losses of almost $100 million to offset capital gains, according to an October 23, 2003, *Wall Street Journal* article. The suit alleges fraud and misrepresentation, among other claims, in connection with a continuing audit of Mandaric's tax returns by the IRS. The suit seeks compensation or losses and costs as well as punitive damages. A BDO spokesman said the claims are without merit.

Adding seven

In May 2003, BDO Seidman expanded its business valuation practice by acquiring seven professionals from Chicago's Investigative Valuation Group, a firm experienced in valuing closely-held companies and consulting on commercial and divorce litigation, estate and gifts, mergers and acquisitions, ESOPs and general business planning. The seven new hires were combined with existing BDO Seidman resources to form a new business valuation and matrimonial consulting group.

GETTING HIRED

Log on to get in

At the careers section of www.bdo.com, job seekers can explore career opportunities at the firm and submit resumes and cover letters online. The site includes a description of the positions (assurance associate, tax associate, and intern) typically offered to recent college graduates. Experienced candidates can search job openings by location and business line, which include assurance, business development, consulting, financial advisory, and internal audit/risk consulting. Additionally, the site lists the benefits offered to employees such as medical, dental and vision insurance, tuition reimbursement, long-term care insurance and flex-time schedules. Regarding the interview process, candidates can expect on-campus screening interviews followed by a round on site, including interviews with partners, managers, and lunches with senior associates. "It wasn't too bad," says one contact from the firm's Westchester county offices.

OUR SURVEY SAYS

Treating you well

"The good thing about BDO is that it is the leader of the middle market," says one insider, who adds, "We have the size, the name and resources, but you are not treated as just another number, which many of my friends in the [Big Four] firms tell me they are." Another source explains, "The upside for members of the firm is that they get a lot of exposure to a number of situations quicker than their counterparts in other firms who focus upon larger Fortune 100 companies."

While one contact characterizes the firm as "pretty conservative," BDO doesn't seem to suffer from stuffiness. Comments one accountant, "For the tax and audit side, I can relate that individuals I have spoken with have reported that the culture seems to be one that is open, fun, hardworking and hard-playing." Another agrees, adding, "The office environment is one of team spirit and camaraderie. "

"The average workweek is around 50 to 55 hours during the busy season and less during the summer," one contact says. Another notes, "You might get screwed now and again and have to work long hours, but personally, I have nothing at all to complain about." Additionally, one contact notes, "You must be open to travel."

Mixing it up

"As for the minority issue," says one source, "I have not seen too many Hispanics or blacks." Another says that "the partnership is probably – although I have no hard numbers – largely white." However, contacts stress that BDO does have an impressive international mix. Says one source, "There are many international staff members throughout the firm." One West Coast contact says, "We have a lot of different employees from all over the world here in L.A."

BKD LLP

Hammons Tower
901 E. St. Louis Street, Suite 1800
P.O. Box 1900
Springfield, MO 65801-1900
Phone: (417) 831-7283
Fax: (417) 831-4763
www.bkd.com

DEPARTMENTS
Accounting
Assurance
Audit
Consulting
Financial Advisory
Tax

THE STATS
Managing Partner: William E. Fingland
Employer Type: Private partnership
Revenue: $215.6 million (FYE 5/03)
No. of Employees: 1,500
No. of Offices: 27

KEY COMPETITORS
Crowe Chizek
Deloitte & Touche
Ernst & Young
KPMG
PricewaterhouseCoopers

UPPERS
- Extensive training and benefits

DOWNERS
- On the cusp of, but still not, the Big Four

EMPLOYMENT CONTACT
Randy Hultz
Career Development Director
Phone: (417) 831-7283
E-mail: rhultz@bkd.com

THE SCOOP

There's no place like Wichita

In 1914, Clinton H. Montgomery, a CPA from Philadelphia, visited Wichita, Kan., to perform an audit on a bankrupt company. Perhaps Montgomery fell in love with the city, or with the oil that had been discovered in the area earlier that year. For whatever reason, he decided to stay in Witchita, where he opened the first public accounting firm in Kansas. Since, Montgomery's firm, the predecessor of BKD (which sets its birth as 1923), has evolved into one of the 10 largest certified public accounting and advisory firms in the U.S. It's also moved its headquarters to Springfield, Mo.

BKD offers consulting, tax, assurance, and accounting outsourcing services. The firm's subsidiaries include BKD Financial, BKD Wealth Advisors, BKD Foundation and Mazars Central. BKD Financial, the group's corporate finance subsidiary, assists companies with mergers, acquisitions, sales, management buyouts, ESOPs, financing and IPO advisory services. It is also a member of the NASD and SIPC. BKD Wealth Advisors provides portfolio management, investment management consulting, financial planning and insurance solutions, and is a registered investment advisor with the Securities and Exchange Commission; the unit manages approximately $500 million for individuals, institutions, trusts and estates. The BKD Foundation is the firm's charitable subsidiary, offering financial support to the communities in which BKD is located. And Mazars Central provides tax assurance and consulting services for multinational companies with business interests in the U.S. Midwest.

Thank you Sarbanes-Oxley

In 2002, the U.S. Congress passed the Sarbanes-Oxley Act, which prevents conflicts of interest between auditors and consultants by prohibiting accounting firms from providing both audit and non-audit services to the same client. (The act also holds executives of public companies responsible for financial reports, and stiffens the penalties against white-collar crime.) The law was enacted in response to energy firm Enron's demise in 2001 and Arthur Andersen's role in the scandal. Under the act, the Big Four accounting firms (Ernst & Young, PricewaterhouseCoopers, KPMG and Deloitte & Touche) have had to pare down their client lists and decide whether to offer auditing or consulting services to their clients. As a result, the smaller regional accounting firms, such as BKD, have reaped the benefits of the new law. In February of 2003, Doug Bennett, director of accounting and auditing at BKD, told CFO.com that after Arthur Andersen filed for bankruptcy, "We saw opportunities for new business and we picked up a few companies." Bennett added that some of the new companies BKD picked up were "just too small for the Big Four."

GETTING HIRED

It's all on there

For everything you ever wanted to know about landing a job at BKD but were afraid to ask, log on to the "career solutions" section of www.bkd.com. There, experienced professionals and recent college graduates can get specifics on BKD jobs, the typical career paths within the firm, the firm's dress code ("Think business first and casual second; wear clean, pressed and wrinkle/stain-free clothing; wear clothing that fits well and is not tight or revealing; choose classic and understated clothing"), employee benefits (the list is long), the extensive training opportunities the firm offers (BKD offers some 15,000 hours of training annually through professional development courses"), interviewing tips and the recruiting process. The site also has a place for candidates to submit a resume online, and includes profiles of current employees as well a description of tasks recent college grads can expect to take on if BKD thinks they have what it takes.

"BKD offers some 15,000 hours of training annually through professional development courses."

— *BKD*

Clifton Gunderson LLP

301 SW Adams Street
Suite 600
Phone: (309) 671-4560
Fax: (309) 671-4576
www.cliftoncpa.com

DEPARTMENTS
Accounting
Assurance
Corporate Finance
Financial Services
International
Management Consulting
Succession Planning
Tax Services
Technology Consulting
Valuation & Forensic

THE STATS
CEO: Carl George
Employer Type: Private partnership
Revenue: $145.0 million (FYE 5/03)
No. of Employees: 1,400
No. of Offices: 52

KEY COMPETITORS
BDO Seidman
Grant Thornton
McGladrey & Pullen
Moss Adams

UPPERS
- Flexible hours

DOWNERS
- Lack of big-time reputation

EMPLOYMENT CONTACT
www.cliftoncpa.com/careers

THE SCOOP

Doing Middle America's taxes

Founded in 1960, Clifton Gunderson is now the 12th-largest professional services firm in the U.S. The firm has 1,400 employees, including more than 500 accountants, in its 52 offices across the country (mostly in the Midwest and Southwest, though the firm goes as far east as Virginia, Maryland and Washington, D.C.). Clifton Gunderson provides typical accounting services like assurance and audit and tax advice as well as management and technology consulting, corporate finance and insurance. The firm also provides services to government agencies in Colorado through its R.S. Wells subsidiary, financial planning and asset management through Clifton Gunderson Financial Services, and additional technology consulting and other tech services through Clifton Gunderson Technology Solutions. Companies and individuals outside the U.S. won't miss out on Clifton Gunderson's services; the firm is a member of HLB International, a consortium of 90 professional services firms that provide advice to international businesses or U.S. companies doing business outside the country.

Clifton Gunderson has recently grown through several recent strategic acquisitions. In June 2003, the firm acquired the Madison, Wis.-based consulting firm Network Technology Solutions. A few months later, Clifton Gunderson upped its capabilities in financial planning, estate planning and business valuation by acquiring accounting firm Coughlin & Mann. The merger, announced in October 2003, adds five new partners and 20 other employees from the Bel Air, Md.-based company.

GETTING HIRED

Keep an eye on your interviewer

Check out Clifton Gunderson's web site, www.cliftoncpa.com, for a detailed career section that has information about benefits, recruiting schedules and processes (both for college hires and lateral recruits) as well as job openings at any of the company's 52 offices. The firm also gives interview tips to prospective applicants (making eye contact and being yourself are encouraged). Clifton Gunderson recruits at nearly 40 schools "mainly in the Midwest." One insider had "three interviews with partners and managers" and "was asked behavioral questions regarding past experiences working in groups."

OUR SURVEY SAYS

It's not all fun and games

Insiders say Clifton Gunderson is "a bit laid-back" and full of "fun people who like to have a good time but take work seriously during business hours." There's no friction between partners and their underlings. "I am treated with respect and my opinions matter," says a tax associate. The firm's compensation structure is typical (though one insider complains that the "pay is low"). In addition to base salary, employees get "a 401(k) with matching," a profit-sharing arrangement and perks that include reimbursement of gym membership fees and payment for educational expenses, including master's degrees and professional training.

Hours are not overwhelming. "There is definitely pressure to get enough charge hours, but I think that is typical of any CPA firm," says one insider. Of course, busy season can be tough. "During tax season, Saturdays are mandatory," says a tax accountant. "The rest of the year, I rarely work on weekends and get quite a bit of paid time off." The firm's commitment to diversity is apparent in its flexible scheduling, which allows for "many part-time mothers" at the firm. "I have moved up the ladder fast," says one female associate, "but I am concerned that there are no female partners in this office."

Vault Guide to the Top Accounting Firms
Clifton Gunderson LLP

"During tax season, Saturdays are mandatory."

— *Clifton Gunderson insider*

Crowe Chizek and Co. LLC

330 East Jefferson Boulevard
South Bend, IN 46624-0007
Phone: (574) 232-3992
Fax: (574) 236-8692
www.crowechizek.com

DEPARTMENTS
Assurance
Consulting
Risk Management
Specialty Services
Tax
Technology

THE STATS
CEO: Mark Hildebrand
Employer Type: Private partnership
Revenue: $247.3 million (FYE 5/03)
No. of Employees: 1,600
No. of Offices: 20

KEY COMPETITORS
BDO Seidman
Clifton Gunderson
McGladrey & Pullen

UPPERS
- Expanding its reach

DOWNERS
- Not a name-brand (Big Four) accountant

EMPLOYMENT CONTACT
Crowe Chizek and Company LLC
Firmwide Recruitment
320 E. Jefferson Blvd.
South Bend, IN 46624
Fax: (574) 236-7609
E-mail: recruiting@crowechizek.com;
campus_recruiting@crowechizek.com

THE SCOOP

Win one for the Gipper

Though it was founded in a town famous for college athletes, there's nothing amateur about Crowe Chizek and Company. Established in South Bend, Ind., the home of college football powerhouse the University of Notre Dame, the professional services firm Crowe Chizek is one of the top 10 accounting firms in the U.S. It has approximately 1,600 employees and 20 offices, mostly in the Midwest and Southeast, and extends its reach outside the U.S. mostly through its membership in Horwath International, a consortium of accounting firms. The firm offers audit and assurance, consulting, risk management, tax, technology, and wealth management services.

Bigger is better

Proving that one man's tragedy is another's victory, Crowe Chizek added to its risk management practice in September 2002, snapping up two risk management partners from the wreckage of what was once Arthur Andersen. Larry Rieger and Rick Julien came to Crowe Chizek from Andersen after that firm collapsed following a conviction on obstruction of justice charges stemming from its representation of energy firm Enron. In January 2003, Crowe Chizek moved into the wealth management game, agreeing to a joint venture with Oxford Financial Group. Crowe Wealth Management will offer investment management and financial planning as well as trust and fiduciary services.

Crowe Chizek added to the fold through acquisition in July 2003, merging with two smaller firms. The firm bought the 50 percent interest it didn't own already in Lake Worth, Fla.-based Carrier & Company, an outsourcing and consulting firm, as part of its strategy of expanding into Florida. Crowe Chizek also announced a merger with Nashville, Tenn.-based Kruse & Associates. The acquisition boosted Crowe Chizek's Tennessee practice (the firm already had an office in Brentwood) and added Kruse & Associates' construction industry expertise.

The July 2003 buying spree was only the latest chapter in Crowe Chizek's expansion plans. In September 2002, the firm acquired Glenview, Ill.-based financial advisor R.V. Norene & Company. In July 2002, the firm purchased an interest in Mexican accounting firm Castillo Miranda, which has offices in three Mexican cities and provides many of the same services as Crowe

Chizek south of the border. The firm also opened a Chicago office in January 2002, moving four partners and 24 staff into a downtown office in the Windy City.

GETTING HIRED

Enlisting in Crowe

Recent and soon-to-be college graduates can apply by sending a resume and cover letter to campus_recruiting@crowechizek.com. Experienced candidates should send their information to recruiting@crowechizek.com, and can also search the firm's careers section of its web site for current openings. The site details all the positions the firm offers in its various departments and includes industries and clients that each department serves, the type of projects each department works on, the role of the staff members, and the training opportunities offered to the staff.

Speaking of training, Crowe Chizek offers an "Audit Boot Camp," where, according to the firm, "extensive classroom training is supplemented with a 'virtual audit.' The course involves competency testing at the end of the program and the training is very project-oriented with you participating in a variety of case studies and role plays that simulate client engagements." Additionally, says the firm, "Tax professionals also attend a vigorous in-house training program" and "all professionals participate in an average of 80 hours of continuing education in the first year and an average of 60 hours each year after."

> "All professionals participate in an average of 80 hours of continuing education in the first year and an average of 60 hours each year after."
>
> — *Crowe Chizek*

Deloitte & Touche LLP

1633 Broadway
New York, NY 10019
Phone: (212) 492-4000
Fax: (212) 492-4154
www.deloitte.com

THE STATS

CEO: James Quigley
Employer Type: Private partnership (U.S. member firm of Deloitte Touche Tohmatsu)
Revenue: $5.9 billion (FYE 6/02)
No. of Employees: 28,203
No. of Offices: 112

KEY COMPETITORS

Ernst & Young
KPMG
PricewaterhouseCoopers

UPPERS

- Flexible hours
- Teamwork-oriented culture

DOWNERS

- Skimping on pay
- Long hours during aptly named busy season

THE SCOOP

Number one

Not long ago Deloitte & Touche sat at the bottom rung of the big accounting firm barrel. Today, though, the American branch of global professional services firm Deloitte Touche Tohmatsu stands as the largest of the Big Four accounting firms (in terms of U.S. revenue). Based in New York City, Deloitte & Touche offers auditing, tax and management consulting services through its offices in more than 80 U.S. cities. In 2003, D&T was named to *Fortune*'s list of the "100 Best Companies to Work for in America" for the sixth consecutive year.

The firm traces its roots back to 1845 when William Welch Deloitte, the grandson of a French count who fled a likely date with the guillotine during the French Revolution, opened an office in London at the age of 25. He first opened for business in the U.S. in 1893. Deloitte's firm merged with Haskins & Sells, a New York-based firm that opened in March 1895. Founders Charles Waldo Haskins and Elijah Watt Sells had met two years earlier when they were tapped by a Congressional commission to investigate operating methods of the executive departments in Washington, D.C. George Touch, who later added the "e" to protect against mispronunciation of his Scottish name, set up shop in 1883. His firm first opened in the U.S. in 1900. Touche Ross (as it became known) merged with Deloitte, Haskins & Sells in December 1989, creating the Big Four behemoth of today.

The last holdout

At the beginning of the new millennium, while other Big Four firms were looking to separate their audit and consulting units, D&T took a different tact. Ernst & Young, responding to regulatory concern regarding a potential conflict of interest, sold its consulting unit in 2000. KPMG spun-off its consulting operation in an IPO in February 2001. And PricewaterhouseCoopers, which announced in January 2002 the spin-off of its consulting services, had been planning a split as early as 2000 (a sale of its consulting unit to Hewlett-Packard fell through in November 2000). Although D&T was receiving several offers for its consulting unit, the firm bucked the trend. "We get calls almost every day," then-CEO Jim Copeland told the *Financial Times* in July 2001. Copeland (who retired in June 2003) rejected the idea that offering consulting and auditing services to the same companies risked a conflict of interest. "As an organization, we have not been distracted by selling out consultancies and dividing the imaginary profits," Copeland said. But come 2002, it appeared as though Copeland and D&T would be forced to change that tune.

In February 2002, while the U.S. Congress was grilling Arthur Andersen on its involvement in the Enron scandal, D&T's parent Deloitte Touche Tohmatsu reluctantly announced that it, too, would be separating its auditing and consulting units. "It's ironic and sad that we are forced by perception to separate our firm," Copeland said during a speech at the National Press Club a few days after the announcement. "This separation will accomplish nothing." Andersen's questionable dealings with Enron forced many to rethink the Big Four common practice of providing both auditing and consulting services to the same client. D&T also announced that it would no longer handle both internal and external auditing for new clients, a move the other Big Four firms had announced previously. Copeland told Reuters, "Now, because of Enron and other high-profile failures, we are forced to dismantle the very model that represents today the best practice in auditing." Deloitte Consulting was to become known as Braxton following the split.

Braxton back in

The separation, however, was not to be. With a poor business climate in the consulting sector and the generally sluggish economy, the partners of the would-be Braxton were unable to raise the financing necessary to move out on their own. In the end, D&T surprised industry observers by announcing its intention to hold on to the consulting unit in April 2003. The firm now finds itself in uncharted waters. In order to avoid violating the Sarbanes-Oxley Act, D&T Consulting must carefully recruit clients that are not clients of the accounting business. Though some analysts are skeptical of the feasibility of this arrangement, D&T officials defend their decision. Deb Harrington, spokeswoman for Deloitte & Touche, is quoted in *Investor's Business Daily* in April 2003 as saying, "We audit 25 percent of U.S. public companies, so the focus of Deloitte Consulting will be on the other 75 percent. We feel pretty confident that we'll be able to maintain independence between the two." Nevertheless, Deloitte's move has already prompted some high profile clients, including General Motors, Clorox and AutoNation, to drop D&T's audit services, consulting services or both.

All talk, no action

For a few days in March 2002, it looked as if Deloitte's parent, Deloitte Touche Tohmatsu, would inherit the messy operations of troubled Big Four Arthur Andersen. Merger negotiations began between the two at about the same time Andersen learned that it faced potential indictment on obstruction of justice in the Enron investigation. *The New York Times* claimed a deal was imminent on March 11, 2002. On the same day, however, *The Wall Street Journal* cautioned against the early call: "The sale or merger effort could come to nothing. It is complicated by the huge liability that Andersen potentially faces for its handling of the Enron audits and the destruction of Enron documents." With Deloitte the second largest of the Big Four in terms of employees, then about half the size of big dog PricewaterhouseCoopers, many thought a Deloitte-Andersen marriage made sense, because the bonded couple could present a serious challenge to PricewaterhouseCoopers. But a few days later, when negotiations between Deloitte and Andersen slowed, reports began circulating that other Big Four firms had jumped into the bidding. Ultimately, Deloitte Touche Tohmatsu, which had been considered Andersen's most likely suitor, withdrew. "We tried to step into this situation with Andersen and be helpful," CEO Copeland told *The New York Times*. "Unfortunately, we were unable to find our way through to a solution." Andersen was convicted of obstruction of justice in June 2002 and after being barred from auditing public companies, ceased operating, turning the Big Five into the Big Four.

From A to D&T

Deloitte & Touche made some nice grabs in 2002 as a result of Arthur Andersen's dissolution. In March 2002, with Andersen facing federal charges for shredding Enron-related documents, Andersen's clients and employees began looking for new homes. Deloitte & Touche, along with fellow big accounting firms PricewaterhouseCoopers, KPMG and Ernst & Young, began picking up ex-Andersen clients and employees. Some of the larger clients that D&T soon inherited include Delta Airlines, United Airlines, International Paper, Hard Rock Hotel, MGM Mirage and Harrah's Entertainment. In the fallout, Deloitte & Touche also hired about 200 ex-Andersen partners in the U.S. to become new tax partners at D&T. The move was a specific attempt by Deloitte & Touche to build its tax-specialty practice in the wake of the Enron scandal and breakup of Andersen. The partners were, for the most part, located in major regions such as Chicago, Atlanta and Dallas.

No love for Adelphia

In June 2002, Pennsylvania-based cable company Adelphia Communications fired Deloitte & Touche as its auditor. The dismissal followed Adelphia's filing for bankruptcy court protection after the firm made disclosures that it had guaranteed about $3 billion in off-balance sheet loans to its founders, the Rigas family. An internal Adelphia investigation revealed that the Rigas family had used the money to build a golf course and to buy stock, timberland and real estate. Adelphia accused D&T of failing to inform Adelphia's audit committee about questionable accounting practices and self-dealings – Deloitte & Touche was not only Adelphia's auditor, but also the Rigas' auditor. The move to fire Deloitte & Touche came amid SEC inquiries into D&T's role in the cable concern's bankruptcy. Following its dismissal, Deloitte & Touche denied wrongdoing, saying Adelphia Communications attempted to withhold important information from auditors and the government, even after a specific committee was created to settle the company's accounting problems. In addition to SEC inquiries, Deloitte & Touche and Adelphia are currently facing several shareholder suits.

Parrett's challenge

Deloitte & Touche grew from the fourth to the second largest accounting firm in the U.S. under the leadership of since-retired CEO James E. Copeland, who also served as the chief executive of parent Deloitte Touche Tohmatsu (DTT grew from the fifth to second spot globally under Copeland). In September 2002, Copeland announced that, at the age of 58, he would take an early retirement the following May to spend more time with his family. On June 1, 2003, William Parrett succeeded Copeland as Global CEO of D&T. Parrett has been with the company for the duration of his 36-year career. He became a partner in the privately held firm in 1977 and served as managing partner of D&T just prior to his promotion. Parrett has stated that his priorities as CEO will be to improve global accounting and auditing standards and to promote corporate accountability. He takes over at a difficult time for the accounting industry, whose integrity has been called into question during the corporate finance scandals of the past couple of years. Deloitte's recent decision to retain its consulting division will further complicate Parrett's job as he attempts to prevent D&T from running afoul of the new industry regulations.

Labor appreciation

Deloitte & Touche is widely recognized as a leader in human resource programs and community involvement. In 2003, for the sixth consecutive year, the firm was named to *Fortune*'s list of the "100 Best Companies to Work for in America." D&T is the only major professional services firm to make the list every year since its inception. In addition, 2003 marked the tenth consecutive year that D&T made *Working Mother* magazine's list of the "100 Best Companies for Working Mothers," an award based on a company's child care services, leave for new parents, flexible work arrangements, work/life benefits and opportunities for women.

Girl power

Among the Big Four, Deloitte & Touche has the highest percentage of female partners and directors, a distinction the firm has held since 1997. In 2003 women accounted for 17 percent of D&T's partners and directors, up from 10 percent in 1997. In the early 1990s, however, the firm's practice of promoting women was anything but praiseworthy. In 1992 only 5 percent of D&T's partners were women. The small number of women in Deloitte's power structure was a factor in the firm's high turnover rate for female employees. In order to understand why women were not represented at the top, in 1993 D&T created the Initiative for the Retention and Advancement of Women, the first such formal program dedicated to retaining and advancing women instituted by a professional services firm. According to D&T, the initiative's task force addressed issues such as why the company had a higher turnover for women than men and why fewer women were being admitted to the partnership. Since the program's inception, the firm has implemented strategies that address advancement, cultural and work/life integration issues. To accelerate female advancement, in 2001 D&T launched Vision 2005, a plan to double the admission rate of high-talent women to partner and director positions. If Vision 2005 is successful, the class of newly admitted partners and directors in 2005 will comprise 35 percent women.

GETTING HIRED

Dept. of pre-identification

Deloitte & Touche works hard to find good candidates before they even know they're candidates. "We constantly strive to identify the best and brightest to hire," says one Deloitte insider. "Many of our more recent hires have been 'pre-identified,' meaning that we identify candidates prior to their final year in college. If a person is not pre-identified by our recruiters, it is much more difficult to receive an offer for full-time employment." In general, the firm's process matches other large accountants. "Like other Big Four firms, Deloitte selects the top students from each of the campuses [at which] it recruits," says one contact. "Typically, only individuals who have high GPAs – usually no lower than 3.3, are actively involved in volunteer student organizations and activities, and have some relevant work experience will make it to the interview process. To actually obtain a job, students will also need to demonstrate good communication skills and the ability to think on their feet." Selectivity can vary with the times. "The firm's selectivity is driven by the economy and quality of graduates in a particular year," according to one source. "When the economy is weak and jobs are difficult to find, the quality of new hires increases. When the economy is strong and jobs for college graduates are more plentiful, the quality of new hires decreases."

"The hiring process typically begins on campus, as Deloitte recruiters will visit campuses or host events for schools," according to one midlevel auditor. "This gives the students and recruiters an informal opportunity to meet and get to know each other. Then at selected time periods, students are required to submit their resumes for the first round of interviews, which are typically conducted on campus with the recruiters or managers of the firm." That insider continues: "The next interview is conducted at one of the firm's offices. Typically, the candidate will meet with a manager, and one or two partners. During both of the interviews, you can expect to be asked behavioral questions." Another auditor tells a similar tale. "Currently the firm performs on-campus interviews," says that contact. "Candidates are interviewed through the 'blitz' style, where they will meet with two different people for approximately 45 minutes. At the end of the day, the interviewers will discuss the various candidates and discuss who will be extended an offer." Another source explains, "The hiring process was very driven by networking with current Deloitte & Touche employees, and the interview process was performed entirely by partners."

Beach or internship?

Summer internships can be a quick ticket to full-time employee. "The experience was great as it allowed me to learn more about the profession and the firm," says one former summer employee. "The work I performed was similar to what full-time, first-year staff would do. Therefore, I was attending client meetings, researching various issues and supporting the various senior members of the engagement team with items they needed assistance on." The contact says the pay was "similar to what a first-year staff would be making." At the end of the internship, the contact was offered a job. "It was an easy decision for me to say yes," adds the source, "as I was much more comfortable and confident with the profession and the firm." The pay is up to par. "I was paid $20 an hour and I did first-year audit work," says a summer veteran. "I think it is much easier to get hired after an internship, because it's like a trial run for the firm and the intern to determine if it's a good match."

OUR SURVEY SAYS

Everybody's pitching in

Insiders find Deloitte & Touche's culture "inclusive and collaborative." Deloitte has "a strong corporate culture," says one source. "Overall, the firm is focused on behaving ethically and responsibly – and this ranges from the services Deloitte performs, to the way Deloitte treats its staff. In an organization of this size, there are always individuals that are exceptions to this, but I believe Deloitte is moving in the right direction." The firm stresses teamwork and cooperation, say its employees. "The culture at Deloitte is very open and supportive," remarks one contact. "There is an open-door policy, meaning that the partners and managers leave their doors open and anyone is able to just drop by to ask questions or just chat. The firm is committed to helping you succeed and when you first start, an informal advisor and a formal advisor – manager or above – are assigned to you." The source adds that these advisors "are there to help mentor you from setting goals to making sure that you are scheduled on the type of clients that you had requested."

Career development is important. "The firm encourages a constant learning environment and a strong support group to your learning," says one insider.

"Early on you are taught by those you work for about the tasks that you need to perform. The firm also sends you to training for at least a week each year. As you move along in the firm you are encouraged to teach those below you as well as to look to those you work with for guidance." That contact continues: "The higher up you get, the more consultative your relationships become with various people within the firm, as they come to you and you go to them with questions. It is more important to know how to get the answer versus knowing the answer, as it is impossible to know everything." In general, most agree that Deloitte fosters a "team environment with a concern about the people. It encourages innovation and strives to recognize high achievers." That doesn't mean there's an excess of handholding. "It is a very fast-paced environment that has little patience for those who cannot keep up," admits another source.

Most at Deloitte express satisfaction with the employee/manager or partner relationship. "Generally, I believe that my managers treat me with respect and allow me flexibility in performing my responsibilities," says one contact who, though, has run into the occasional problem. "Since we work with and for different people with different personalities, there have been occasions when I have had difficulty working with certain individuals." Others warn about the aberrational jerk. "Some people are very friendly and open-minded and then you have the really immature ones," observes one source.

Those fluctuating hours

Hours at Deloitte are typical of Big Four firms, but like many Big Four employees, Deloitte insiders wish for a little more consistency. "Hours are seasonal and fluctuate week-to-week," says one contact. "I don't consistently work 50 to 60 hours each week. I work 40 one week, 60 the next, etc." "Peaks and valleys are embedded in our office due to the nature of our business, and the peaks can become more frequent depending upon client needs and expectations," agrees another source. "Charge hours are frequently stressed. However, as I have not had problems meeting my expected level of chargeability I have not felt pressure in this area."

Things can get a little hectic around the firm's busiest time. "Busy season has a minimum of 50 to 55 hours per week and it runs from January through March," reports one insider. Of course, things can get busy out-of-season as well. "Also, if you are on an engagement that has a year-end other than the calendar year, you may work the busy season hours." Things seem to improve as you move up the ladder. "There is a lot of flexibility in the time we spend as you move up in the organization," says one source. "The firm has moved to the virtual office, which means that you can work from anywhere at anytime. Depending upon what your client's needs are, this gives you the ability, on occasion, to work from home at times that are convenient to you. The offset to this is being available to people and their having the ability to track you down when needed."

Pay problems

Some insiders think Deloitte is frugal when it comes to compensating its employees. "I feel there is a compression issue at my firm," says one source. "Since the market for new accounting students is weak, they receive a higher base starting salary, which isn't too far from the salaries of people who've been with the firm one to three years." Other complaints exist. "Public accounting used to be known for its large raises, because employees work extreme amounts of hours compared to our peers in industry," according to one auditor. "Now, however, raises are the same as those in other industries. My salary was higher than my peers when I graduated. Now our salaries are comparable, and I am still working more hours than my peers." Help may be on the way. One insider reports that a "new compensation structure rolled out for 2004 will significantly change salary and bonus."

If the new regime doesn't make things all right, unsatisfied accountants have options. "After spending a few years at the firm and obtaining your certification, private industry will always pay more than what the firm is paying," says one source. "My understanding is that we are one of the lowest paid within the Big Four."

Getting to know things

In general, Deloitte & Touche accountants are satisfied with the firm's training initiatives. "I am provided with ample opportunities to learn," says one source. "We are sent to formal training for one week out of the year," reports another contact. "The training is conducted at Deloitte's training facility in Scottsdale, Arizona. There are many more opportunities for training in the local office during the course of the year." "The firm really strives to constantly educate you on items you need to know," says one insider. "There is a week of training offsite. The national office works towards identifying what skills people need at various levels."

Praise for diversity

Deloitte is making an effort to recruit and retain qualified female accountants, say sources. "We are really focusing on the advancement and retention of women," brags one insider. Indeed, the firm has formal programs to foster diversity, both in terms of gender and ethnicity. "Deloitte is focused on the Women's Initiative and appears to be making good progress in hiring, promoting and mentoring women," says one source. "The firm's initiative for the Retention and Advancement of Women receives high visibility within the firm and externally," says another contact. Similar efforts are being made to find and keep minorities at Deloitte. "The firm seems to be concerned with and receptive to hiring and promotion of minorities," says one source. "However, implementation is slow and seems very difficult."

"It is a very fast-paced environment that has little patience for those who cannot keep up."

– Deloitte & Touche insider

Ernst & Young LLP

5 Times Square
New York, NY 10036
Phone: (212) 773-3000
www.ey.com

THE STATS

Chairman and CEO: James S. Turley
Employer Type: Private partnership (U.S. member firm of Ernst & Young International)
Revenue: $4.5 billion (FYE 6/02)
No. of Employees: 23,000
No. of Offices: 95

KEY COMPETITORS

Deloitte & Touche
KPMG
PricewaterhouseCoopers

UPPERS

- Top-notch reputation
- Super treatment by superiors

DOWNERS

- Low bonuses
- Can be bureaucratic

THE SCOOP

IRS v. E&Y

Ernst & Young LLP is the U.S. member firm of Ernst & Young Global Ltd., one of the Big Four global professional services organizations with 103,000 employees stationed throughout 140 countries. Ernst & Young audits over 100 of the Fortune 500 companies and has consistently posted double-digit growth and led its competitors in tax services and technology.

The firm, though, has experienced its share of setbacks; most notably the company has been targeted by a spate of lawsuits and accusations of conflicts of interest as it struggles to reconcile concurrent auditing and consulting relationships with certain clients. Some of its most widely publicized troubles involve communications giant Sprint. An investigation by the Internal Revenue Service into the firm's relationship with Sprint raised questions about tax shelter advice E&Y had given to the communications company and other clients. Ernst & Young had provided tax shelter advice to two high-ranking Sprint executives while also serving as the corporation's auditor. In July 2003, Ernst & Young and the IRS agreed to a financial settlement regarding the Sprint matter. Sprint has since ended its audit relationship with Ernst & Young. But such regulatory problems have been plaguing the accounting industry in general, not just E&Y. A similar settlement had already been reached between the IRS and PriceWaterhouseCoopers; federal suits are still underway against two other accounting firms, KPMG and BDO Seidman.

The silver lining

Even with all its troubles, the firm has experienced some bright spots. In April 2002, E&Y moved into its new, 37-floor U.S. headquarters at 5 Times Square in New York; the firm expects to grow its Manhattan staff from 4,600 to approximately 6,000. And in May 2002, the firm began a significant expansion of its global reach, adding new offices and hundreds of former Andersen employees, including many former partners.

At heart, a nice Midwestern firm

Ernst & Young's history goes back more than a century, to the 1890s in Chicago. At that time, many benighted American businesses had no notion of regulated accounting practice, and the government had yet to burden

American taxpayers with the income tax. English businesses based in the United States, however, knew better, and sent for British-trained Scottish accountants to look after their investments. One enterprising Scotsman, Arthur Young, set up an independent accounting firm in Chicago in 1894. This firm became Arthur Young & Company in 1906. Meanwhile, two brothers, A.C. and Theodore Ernst, Americans who had been quick to pick up on the accounting concept, launched a tiny accounting firm in Cleveland in 1903. A.C. Ernst had previously worked for the CEO of a large industrial firm and believed that accounting could be used to help corporate management make smarter, money-saving decisions.

Arthur Young and Ernst & Ernst got a large bounce in 1913, when the passage of the federal income tax suddenly created big business for tax departments. Arthur Young, growing steadily, formed a national partnership in 1921, uniting its five offices behind its new headquarters in New York City. Ernst & Ernst's expansion and promotion hit a snag in the early 1930s, when the American Institute of Certified Public Accountants (AICPA) adopted a policy prohibiting members from advertising. For a time, A.C. Ernst resigned from the association. Still, the financial chaos of the 1930s proved to be lucrative for both Arthur Young and Ernst & Ernst, as the Great Depression spawned new financial reporting regulations that increased the need for accounting and auditing services. To snare enough employees to meet demand that decade, Arthur Young began to recruit college students and to train them in its first staff school.

Both firm patriarchs went to their heavenly reward in 1948; Arthur Young at 84, and A.C. Ernst at the relatively young age of 66. Arthur Young (the firm) made news in 1957 by appointing the first female partner in what was then the Big Eight, and Ernst & Ernst merged with British firm Whinney, Murray & Co. to become Ernst & Whinney. Finally, Arthur Young and Ernst & Whinney found each other, merging in 1989 to become Ernst & Young.

The merger that wasn't

With the creation of Citigroup, DaimlerChrysler and others, the year 1998 will no doubt be remembered as a vintage one for mergers. But a sour note was the failed union between Ernst & Young and what was then KPMG Peat Marwick (now called KPMG). Announced in October 1997, the deal would have created the world's largest professional services organization, with thousands of partners worldwide and $18 billion in total revenue. At the time of the announcement, neither company anticipated trouble – not only had KPMG and Ernst & Young helped numerous corporations negotiate the pitfalls of the merger process, they were also themselves the products of important mergers in the accounting industry. However, this deal faced heightened scrutiny from antitrust regulators, as various government agencies, notably the Department of Justice and the European Union Merger Task Force, had recently begun to question why profits at the biggest professional services firms were increasing as fees remained flat. Given the prospect of regulatory inquiries in the United States, Japan, Europe, Canada and Australia, KPMG and E&Y called off the transaction in February 1998, stating that the merger "would have taken many months, incurring considerable costs and potentially considerable disruption to client service."

Other observers, however, noted that regulatory issues weren't the only reason the merger failed. In particular, some argued that internal disputes had derailed the deal. Arthur Bowman, editor of *Bowman's Accounting Report*, found it hard to believe that two major accounting firms had neglected to consider the costs of government scrutiny, and commented to *The Washington Post*, "They're using the regulatory process as their excuse for not merging." Instead, Bowman said, "the concept of the merger was driven by the U.S. partners – it caused a lot of anguish outside the [United] States."

Whatever the reason for the deal's failure, the fact that KPMG and E&Y remained separate certainly helped open the door for Price Waterhouse and Coopers & Lybrand, whose merger passed regulatory muster and reduced the Big Six to the Big Five. One mega-merger is apparently easier to take than two.

Face to face with the Feds

Like all the big accounting firms, Ernst & Young was forced to defend itself in 2002 against charges of questionable or biased audits. In one case, the SEC investigated E&Y for its audit of Cendant Corp. The SEC questioned E&Y's practice of giving Cendant price breaks on its audits in exchange for consulting business. The commission also later warned three Ernst & Young auditors that they could face civil charges for their role in the Cendant audit. Additionally, *The Wall Street Journal* reported that E&Y's audit materials for Computer Associates were subpoenaed, and that E&Y was under investigations for transactions it promoted and approved for PNC Financial Services Group Inc.

In another case, an SEC commissioner charged E&Y in May 2002 with violating auditor independence rules by marketing and installing products made by PeopleSoft, a Pleasanton, Calif.-based software maker and Ernst &

Young client. The SEC wanted the firm to terminate the marketing agreement and return fees for auditing work done during the agreement. E&Y denied that its sales relationship was improper, and argued that a single SEC commissioner couldn't authorize an enforcement action. The SEC went ahead with the E&Y investigation based on the vote of only one member, rather than a quorum of at least two members. This ultimately led to the case's dismissal in July 2002, when an administrative law judge threw it out, saying the SEC improperly instituted the suit by going ahead with only one vote.

Ernst & Young's string of good luck in the courtroom continued into 2003 as the firm appeared to dodge another legal bullet. The Federal Deposit Insurance Corporation (FDIC) had filed a lawsuit against E&Y in November 2002 in connection with the firm's audit of Superior Bank, which federal regulators seized in one of the largest banking failures in 10 years. The FDIC suit accused Ernst & Young of fraud and gross negligence, claiming that Ernst & Young's head office in New York knew of accounting improprieties at Superior, but that it failed to disclose them until after selling its consulting division to Cap Gemini. Ernst & Young didn't want the negative publicity while it was trying to sell the unit, the suit maintained. The FDIC, which paid out more than $750 million from its insurance fund because of Superior Bank's failure, was looking to claim more than $2 billion in compensatory and punitive damages from the Big Four firm. The regulators indicated they were seeking such a large sum because Ernst & Young had a history of regulatory offenses. The suit was filed by the FDIC in its "corporate capacity" rather than as receiver of Superior Bank. But in April 2003, a federal judge dismissed the suit, ruling that the agency had no standing to sue Ernst & Young in their corporate capacity. Its only legal claim against E&Y was as receiver of Superior's assets. Since the contract signed between Ernst & Young and Superior's managers provided for a mandatory arbitration procedure to settle disputes, the judge ruled that the FDIC was obliged to bring the complaint before an arbitrator, a process that prohibits the award of punitive damages. In May 2003, FDIC officials announced their intention to appeal the ruling.

One's pains are another's gains

Following Andersen's June 2002 conviction on obstruction of justice charges related to the Enron collapse, the *Los Angeles Times* called Ernst & Young the "biggest winner from Andersen's meltdown, gaining 189 former Andersen clients, or more than a quarter of the business that has defected from the troubled accounting firm." According to the *Los Angeles Times*, the new E&Y

clients accounted for $300 million of Andersen's $4 billion in U.S. revenue for 2001. Among the new clients are several huge hotel chains, including Hilton Hotels, Marriott International, Westin Hotels and Starwood Hotels & Resorts Worldwide. Ernst & Young also gained about 200 partners and 1,000 staff members in key regions such as New York, Los Angeles and Baltimore. In addition, E&Y agreed to take over 54 of Andersen Worldwide's 83 overseas partnerships.

Light at the end of the tunnel

There are signs now that Ernst & Young, and indeed the whole of the accounting industry, may finally be emerging from the cloud of scandals that has plagued it since 2001. Though the consequences from the deluge of misconduct allegations that emerged in 2001 and 2002 have yet to fully play out, Ernst & Young appears to be on the road to recovery. The firm scored a legal victory in February 2003 when a British judge dismissed the majority of the claims brought against it by failed insurance company Equitable Life, which claimed that E&Y had negligently failed to inform company officials of the insurance firm's shaky financial situation. The insurer was originally seeking £2.6 billion in damages; ultimately the judge permitted a smaller claim of £500 million to proceed. The Court of Appeals in the U.K. reinstated the case in July 2003, but in doing so, indicated skepticism in its written opinion.

In June 2003, Ernst & Young announced sweeping internal reforms meant to clean up the company's accounting practices and improve its reputation. Some of the concrete steps announced by the company include a 40 percent increase in the technical staff that works on complex audit projects, the cessation of services such as operational audits that have been outlawed by the new Sarbanes-Oxley Act, and a new code of conduct that each member of Ernst & Young must now sign and uphold.

Finally, in July 2003, Ernst & Young agreed to a settlement with the Internal Revenue Service (IRS), which had been conducting an investigation into tax shelter abuse. Under the terms of the agreement, E&Y agreed to pay $15 million in fines and to cooperate with IRS investigators by providing the names of clients who may be employing tax shelters to evade income tax.

Treating you well

In January 2003, E&Y was named to *Fortune*'s "100 Best Companies to Work For," a list of firms that best help employees balance their work and personal lives. It was the company's fifth consecutive appearance in the annual rankings. In the 2002 rankings, *Fortune* reported that one of the reasons a company makes the list is its "willingness ... to scramble to come up with creative ways to keep employees satisfied and to treat them with respect and dignity." For E&Y, "that meant redeploying people" and "offering voluntary leaves of absence at 25 percent of pay." The 2003 survey cited domestic partner benefits and two weeks of paid leave for new mothers and fathers as prime perks.

Ernst & Young also has been named to *Working Mother*'s "100 Best Companies for Working Mothers" list for four straight years, from 1999 to 2002. The firm also landed on *Training* magazine's 2002 "Training Top 100," snagging the No. 7 spot for its training and education programs.

GETTING HIRED

Calling all college students

Ernst & Young "welcomes applications from candidates at all schools," so interested parties should check with the career services office at their school. "I had three rounds of interviews before I got my offer," reports one insider. "The first interview was on campus, and the others were on-site to meet with staff and partners. In total I probably met with 15 people." That contact was impressed with the people he encountered. "I thought the interview process was very objective. The people who interviewed me were professional, yet personable – this is what really attracted me to the company." Another auditor remembers "basic interview questions" in his first round including such nuggets as, "Tell me a time when you worked in a successful team, demonstrated leadership, etc."

In later rounds, that source recalls meeting with a partner to talk about "fit with the firm and life at E&Y." According to another contact, questions that might pop up include: "Can you recall a time when you made a mistake? Explain the circumstances and what you did to fix the problem" and "Recall a time when you worked as a team and a team member wasn't pulling their load." Bring your social skills and your appetite. "I met with one partner, two senior managers and went out to lunch with two other staff people," says one accountant. "The interview with the partner and senior managers lasted approximately 30 minutes each and were behavioral in nature."

OUR SURVEY SAYS

Split on culture

Insiders have varied opinions on the company's culture. "Ernst & Young is actually a great place to work," says an auditor. "In our group the people are extremely close and create an open environment to work well in. Most partners have an open-door policy and are easily accessible." "Working at Ernst & Young has been an extremely enjoyable and rewarding experience for me," says another insider. "The company really focuses on putting its people first. Everyone here works really long hours, but the culture does not mandate face time. I often work from home or come in late or leave early, and no one ever gives me a hard time." Some feel the firm has a relaxed atmosphere. "The culture is pretty laid-back, except during busy season, which starts from December and ends in April."

But Ernst & Young has its critics, and they are vocal. "If you are seeking a company that maintains high morale and boosts its employees, this is not the place for you," warns one contact. "While there are always pros and cons to working for a large corporation, and especially the subsidiary of a large corporation, the cons outweigh the pros in this instance." One con is vast bureaucracy. "As I suspect any Big Four is, [Ernst & Young is] very hierarchical." The effects of the bureaucracy are felt far and wide. "Transferring between departments is much more difficult than it should be," observes one source. The firm has worked on the problem but apparently to no avail. "E&Y is bureaucratic and a boys' club," complains one source. "A few years ago, our firm culture was identified by external consultants as being centered first on the firm, second on clients and last on people. Our new PeopleFirst initiative is supposed to realign the culture but most employees consider the initiative to be a joke." Like any big company, Ernst & Young has its share of office politics. One contact says, "On a number of occasions, I've overheard things like, 'No, I don't want to work with him because he showed up late to a meeting once,' or 'No, she works in the New York office.' Unprofessionalism under a guise of professionalism is the norm in this culture."

OK on pay, hurting on bonuses

At Ernst & Young, "salaries are competitive, but not overly generous." The firm "has a salary range for each level," according to one source. "Analysts receive a base salary of between $45,000 and $50,000 nationwide, regardless of cost of living. So if you want to be in New York, consider this very carefully as it means your rent will most likely be half of your monthly take-home pay." "Bonuses are very limited," warns an insider, who adds, "don't expect anything." While E&Y gets high marks from some on its benefit offerings, others in the firm see them as sub-par. "Benefits at E&Y are poor because a large employee contribution is required," says one insider. Going back to school can be an option. "Tuition reimbursement is available," reports one employee. "I found that people in tax had better luck obtaining this than [those in] auditing." The company has a generous vacation policy with up to three weeks, in addition to personal days for new hires, but you'd better get it done before the end of the year because "if you are on a project and are unable to take your vacations, it's tough, luck, Charlie."

Back to school

Praise abounds for E&Y's training program. "The firm has really good training programs. They expect you to come in with a certain amount of knowledge, but they offer a lot," explains one contact. "We encourage everyone to manage their own career," says another. One source adds, "If you find a program you're interested in, there's not much red tape to go through." Another insider describes a variety of classes ranging from software training to language classes.

"Most partners have an open-door policy and are easily accessible."

— *Ernst & Young insider*

Grant Thornton LLP

175 West Jackson Boulevard
20th Floor
Chicago, IL 60604
Phone: (312) 856-0001
Fax: (312) 565-4719
www.grantthornton.com

THE STATS

CEO: Edward E. Nusbaum
Employer Type: Private partnership (U.S. operation of Grant Thornton International)
Revenue: $459.0 million (FYE 12/03)
No. of Employees: 3,269
No. of Offices: 49

DEPARTMENTS

Assurance and Advisory Services
Compensation and Benefits
International
M&A Advisory Services
Management Advisory Services
Tax Consulting Services
Valuation Services

KEY COMPETITORS

Deloitte & Touche
Ernst & Young
KPMG
PricewaterhouseCoopers

UPPERS

- Exemplary culture
- Flexible schedules in down times

DOWNERS

- Compensation not up to par
- Rough hours around tax-filing season

EMPLOYMENT CONTACT

Visit the "careers" section of the firm's web site:
www.grantthornton.com/careers

THE SCOOP

Old-timers

Grant Thornton is the top accounting firm in the U.S. that serves middle-market companies (those with revenues ranging between $50 million and $1 billion), and the country's fifth largest accountant in terms of revenue, remaining just outside the industry's inner circle called the Big Four. Based in Chicago, this formidable firm's history spans 80 years. In 1924, 26-year-old Alexander Grant founded an eponymous accounting firm in the Windy City. In its first decades, the firm grew slowly, gaining speed through the 1960s as it expanded internationally.

In 1980, Alexander Grant & Company helped form and became a member of Grant Thornton International, an umbrella organization that today has 585 member and affiliate offices in 110 countries around the world, with 21,500 employees and nearly $2 billion in annual global revenue; Grant Thornton International is one of six global accounting organizations. In 1986, Alexander Grant & Company changed its name to Grant Thornton. The firm added the LLP to its moniker in 1995 when it became a limited liability partnership. Today, Grant Thornton has 319 partners in 49 offices across the U.S.

Breaking it down

In addition to being divided by service, the firm is also divided by industry. The following is a list of the firm's industry lines: construction, real estate and hospitality; consumer and industrial products; financial services; global public sector; government contractors; not-for-profit sectors; and technology. Two of the most visible of Grant Thornton's industry concentrations are headquartered outside the Midwest. The financial services division is based in New York and provides clients with specialized accounting and business advisory services to the brokerage, investment, foreign banking, and mortgage banking sectors. And Grant Thornton's global public sector unit, headquartered in Washington, D.C., works with local, state, federal and international governments.

AA fallout

The firm, like other accounting concerns, profited from Arthur Andersen's downfall, absorbing a number of that company's employees and offices since

June 2002. Grant Thornton picked up former Arthur Andersen staffers and offices in Charlotte, Greensboro and Raleigh, N.C., Columbia, S.C., Milwaukee, Detroit, New York, Orlando, Albuquerque, Cleveland, Cincinnati, Tampa, Tulsa, San Francisco and Vienna, Va. All told, those acquisitions added 60 partners and more than 550 employees to Grant Thornton's staff. Additionally, in January 2003, the company acquired Brueggeman and Johnson PC, a Seattle-based valuation firm. Fueled in part by these acquisitions, Grant Thornton has been gearing up to make a name for itself. In January 2003, it placed second in *Public Accounting Report*'s quarterly audit ratings – the first time a non-Big Four (Andersen was by then defunct) firm had placed in the top two. The rankings measure the largest net gain in revenue for the quarter. For fiscal year 2003, Grant Thornton announced record revenue growth, boosting sales by 25 percent to $459 million.

Taking the high road

In September 2003, Grant Thornton announced it would cease to provide certain services to its audit clients, even though the services aren't banned under the Sarbanes-Oxley Act of 2002. The move was a preemptive one in order to avoid any potential conflicts of interest. It was also a move that other big accounting firms don't plan to follow. In a press release, Grant Thornton said it would not design, document or evaluate internal controls for its public audit clients. (Internal controls are designed to safeguard assets or to prevent or detect problems ranging from accounting errors to security breaches.) In that same release, Grant Thornton CEO Ed Nusbaum said, "There are areas in the legislation that are clear, and some that might be interpreted differently by others. But the guide in gray areas should be in the spirit of reform and protection of investors that the bill's authors intended." Nusbaum added that if clients "need assistance in documenting their internal controls, we will inform them of other options that are available."

GETTING HIRED

Grades matter

It's tough to get hired at Grant Thornton, and it's tougher thanks to a rough economy and the company's relatively small size. "Our firm is committed to hiring talented, intelligent individuals enthusiastic about a career in accounting with a middle-market firm," says one insider. "Not only do we require excellent grades, we look for well-rounded individuals," says another contact. "We also hire fewer individuals than the Big Four so there is less likelihood of getting hired." GPA is a factor, and so are the tests you fretted over in high school but thought were way behind you. "If you do not have at least a 3.2 GPA, and more like a 3.5, and fairly high ACT and SAT scores, you are not even considered," warns one contact. "Additionally, you must typically show many extracurricular activities and/or job experience." Being CPA-eligible is, naturally, important. "I believe the firm looks for outstanding individuals with exceptional personalities," according to one accountant. "Main criteria include GPA and CPA eligibility."

Meeting management

The recruiting process at Grant Thornton usually starts with seemingly innocent on-campus events. "The college recruiting process is as follows: Students are met and preselected for interviews – both internship and full time – at the various recruiting events sponsored by the school," says one tax associate. "They are then interviewed by a manager or partner, generally from the office they desire to work in. Based on those interviews, candidates are chosen for office visits, where they meet the partner, two to three managers, four to five senior/staff associates that they will be working with." Offers are then made based on the office visit recommendations. As for experienced hires, they're "interviewed by the three to four managers and two to three partners they will be working with most often," says an insider, "and possibly the regional managing partner, depending on the position they are interviewing for."

Things can also get rolling with a phone interview. "The hiring process usually involves several phone discussions and screenings, followed by a general informational meeting, followed by a first round of interviews, followed by a second round of interviews, followed by a decision," reports one insider. Expect to see more partners than the average firm. "One thing that is very different at Grant Thornton from other accounting firms' hiring process is that the partners take the lead," says one audit associate. "They are doing the interviewing and making sure we hire the best. Generally, candidates will meet with an HR person, a partner, a manager, and maybe a senior." Questions range from technical to more getting-to-know-you. "Among questions asked was 'Why did I choose accounting as my major?' and 'Where do I see myself in five years?'" recalls one insider. Another source remembers the following queries: "[I was] asked about technical background in international tax and about professional aspirations."

Spring, not summer, internships

Accounting firms generally hire fewer interns than most companies in the summer; that's because they need help in the spring to meet tax filing deadlines. "They do not have a summer internship, but they do have a spring or busy season internship, which was great because I was treated as any other first-year associate," recalls one contact. "They paid $16 per hour plus overtime." "Our internships are typically in the spring," says one source. "The pay scale is typically that of a new associate. The work experience is the same as if the candidate were a full-time new hire. Unless performance issues are apparent during the internship, the hiring process is typically much easier afterward."

OUR SURVEY SAYS

Accountant's paradise

Insiders say Grant Thornton is a "friendly and understanding" firm with "high expectations for work ethic, moral ethics and firm commitment. [The] people are patient and willing to help." "Firm culture is wonderful," glows another insider. "Everyone from partner to staff is friendly and easy to work with. It is truly a family environment." The firm has a different feel than the larger accountants. "Grant Thornton is a more open environment compared to Big Four firms," says one Houston insider. "As a smaller office, it allows you to make a name for yourself, and be involved in areas that you normally would not be [like] recruiting, research, planning company events, training development, etc." Small offices seem to be the place to go. "At our office, the people are very friendly and we all get along very well," says a Reno accountant. "I have never had a problem that I couldn't discuss with a manager or partner. We're rather casual and quite flexible."

Others at Grant Thornton praise the firm's small-firm feel while saluting its international prestige. "I believe our office works much like a family where everyone knows each other, and we are all on a first name basis. However, the firm itself is tremendous." A tremendous firm expects tremendous results. "At Grant Thornton there is an expectation of excellence with acknowledgement of a job well done," says a contact. "It's a very friendly, congenial atmosphere in a firm that has a well-articulated mission to be the leader in its middle-market niche." Grant Thornton's sudden expansion is putting some strain on the firm's culture. "It is a family-oriented firm in a growth mode that is feeling some pain from this growth," says a source. "However, the firm is heading in the right direction and is growing within normal bounds."

Grant Thornton allows for business casual dress, except when meeting with clients. "I have yet to wear a tie," brags one source. "We are business appropriate," explains an insider. "While at a client we dress the way they do. When we are at the office it is business casual." You'll have to keep your Levi's at home. "We used to be able to wear jeans on Fridays, but we can't anymore," says a contact.

Getting the respect you deserve

"Our management team generally treats everyone well," observes one insider. "On rare occasions we have had individuals on the management team that have been politically motivated, but that is the exception and not the rule." Others support that observation. "In general, our managers treat us with respect," says a source. "However, there are times when managers talk down to subordinates or expect more than is reasonable based on the level of experience." Grant Thornton seems to have an open-door policy. "Our culture is such that anyone can approach another member of the firm, regardless of their position in the corporate hierarchy, to chat, discuss a client matter, etc.," says an associate.

Hurting on payday

Grant Thornton's compensation scheme has its critics. "The pay is right on pace with the rest of the industry" to start. But then things get dicey. "I believe our salary increases are not comparable to the Big Four accounting firms at this point in time," gripes one accountant. The firm has a pretty strict method of determining pay. "Compensation and bonus are set at the beginning of the year in our performance assessment tool and monitored throughout the year," reports a source. Bonuses are a source of complaint. "[The] bonus program is unfair," fumes a contact, though others say the firm rewards top performers and "additional one-time bonuses are also available for 'above and beyond' effort and accomplishments." There are other problems. "Benefits here are not up to par, only half of licensing and association fees are covered by the firm even though the license is required and associations are strongly recommended," complains one insider. "Also, health benefits are more expensive to the employee than I would have expected." On the bright side, there is a "good 401(k) plan." However, effective August 1, 2003, Grant Thornton introduced a new bonus plan based on employee and partner feedback. According to the firm, "The new plan focuses on overall performance and enhances the role of coaches. In addition, top performers at the firm have a chance at an increased bonus award."

Say goodbye to spring

Like any accounting firm, Grant Thornton employees rarely see the simple beauty of flowers blooming and robins returning. "Hours are very good," says one insider. "As with all accounting firms we have our busy season where we are required to work an abundance of hours. However, during the summer and off periods the firm is wonderful with being flexible about work hours." Weekends are a virtual requirement during the busy season. "We are required to work every Saturday during busy season, and if we don't come in on Saturday, it is a big deal," says one accountant. The difference between the busy season and the rest of year is substantial. "During the non-busy season times it is usually normal 40-hour weeks," reports one contact. "When it is busy, the total hours are usually between 50 and 60." Things have gotten worse. "Every year for the past three to four years the billable hours goals have seemed to rise," says a contact. "I still work fewer hours than my friends at the Big Four but I regret many of the emergency hours that come with my profession." Even non-accountants aren't protected from the hour crunch. "There is a large amount of pressure to bill at the firm, with billing being a primary goal," says one insider. "Since my unit [valuation services] is heavily focused on consulting, long hours are needed as the project demands."

The next wave in training

Not everyone loves Grant Thornton's new training system. "The firm has required training sessions," says an insider. "They promote training firm-wide through the use of GT University. All courses are online and provide direct and immediate interaction with students from other cities and faculty. Sessions can be viewed live or a student can replay a previously recorded session." The computerized training isn't perfect. "I miss the national training in Chicago that used to be the norm," says a source. "Now, most of our training is via Centra, which doesn't allow for the social interaction/networking with staff from other offices. The amount of topics and level of training through Centra is very good though." "[I] think that it would be nice to have a brown bag lunch with people that have experience and can share their expertise," says an accountant. Some blast the web-based system completely. "I went to a new hire training, which was terrible," says one insider. But there are other ways to learn your stuff. The source admits that "on-the-job training and local office training has been great."

Making strides on diversity

Insiders are pretty pleased with Grant Thornton's diversity efforts. "The firm has policies in place to promote the respect of diversity of the employees and protect individuals from bias or discrimination," says one insider. "The company is very open to hiring and promoting women," according to one source. "Also, women with families are allowed to travel less if desired. Schedules are flexible to each employee's needs." Female employees seem to move to part-time schedules, insiders observe. "We seem to hire quite a few women, but after time, they want to work part time and not travel as much," says a contact.

"To my knowledge, there is no distinction between ethnic groups – minorities or otherwise – in the workplace whatsoever," says one source. "There are several individuals of different ethnicities in our manager and partner ranks, as people of all ethnicities appear to be given the same opportunities for advancement and recognition." The firm may not have had all the success it wants. "We are trying but have a small number of minorities at all levels," observes one contact.

KPMG LLP

345 Park Avenue
New York, NY 10154
Phone: (212) 758-9700
Fax: (202) 758-9819
www.kpmg.com

THE STATS

Chairman and CEO: Eugene D. O'Kelly
Employer Type: Private partnership (U.S. arm of KPMG International)
Revenue: $3.42 billion (FYE 9/02)
No. of Employees: 17,700

KEY COMPETITORS

Deloitte & Touche
Ernst & Young
PricewaterhouseCoopers

UPPERS

- Big Four prestige
- Chance to snag a big bonus with good reviews

DOWNERS

- Hellacious hours
- Nickel-and-dime culture keeps an eagle eye on expense accounts

EMPLOYMENT CONTACT

www.kpmgcareers.com

THE SCOOP

Where the urge to merge began

Of the accounting firms that once made up the industry's Big Eight, only four remain. And in some ways, KPMG has played a pivotal role in creating this new landscape. The first of the so-called "mega mergers" between accounting firms took place in 1987 when Peat Marwick International (PMI) and Klynveld Main Goerdeler (KMG) joined forces.

KPMG, the most internationally oriented of the major accountancies, operates in three global business units: Europe/Middle East/Africa, Asia/Pacific, and the Americas (operating under the name KPMG LLP in the U.S.). The firm offers professional services such as assurance, tax, legal and financial advice. Notably absent from KPMG's slate of service offerings is consulting. In 2001, the company's consulting division was spun off; today, it goes by the name BearingPoint.

Menu of services

KPMG's services in the U.S. fall into one of two main categories: assurance and tax. The assurance practice advises its clients on ways to monitor, manage and mitigate risk. Services offered by the assurance group include audit, forensic accounting services, corporate recovery advice and transaction (i.e. merger and acquisition) advisory services. KPMG's tax practice, meanwhile, helps companies find and realize tax savings by optimizing their corporate structures. The firm employs specialists in international trade; customs regulations; and federal, state and local tax codes. KPMG also dispenses legal services through an independent but affiliated network of law firms called KLegal International, which employs more than 2,500 lawyers in 50 countries, primarily in Europe, Asia and Latin America.

Industry expertise

KPMG organizes their various services into multidisciplinary teams focused on individual industry sectors so as to better understand each client's business. These sectors are further grouped into five lines of business: financial services; information, communications and entertainment; industrial markets; consumer markets; and health care and public sector. In the financial services field, KPMG has teams working in the banking and finance, insurance and real estate sectors. The information, communications and entertainment group includes the software, electronics, and communications and media teams. Within industrial markets are the industrial and automotive products; chemicals and pharmaceuticals; energy, power and natural resources; and transportation sectors. The consumer markets group offers teams specializing in consumer products, retail and food and beverage. Finally, in the health care and the public sector group, teams are assigned to cover health care providers, federal government, state and local government, higher education and non-profit organizations.

Follow the merging accountants

Today's KPMG was built through a series of partnerships, alliances and mergers dating back to the turn of the 20th century. The oldest piece of the KPMG puzzle, William Barclay Peat & Company, was founded by William Barclay Peat in London in 1870. Across the Atlantic in New York City, James Marwick and Roger Mitchell created Marwick, Mitchell and Company nine years later. In 1911 Peat and Marwick entered into a business alliance. The relationship was formalized as an official merger in 1925, creating Peat, Marwick, Mitchell and Copartners. The firm changed its name to Peat Marwick International (PMI) in 1978.

KMG, meanwhile, was created by the merger of several (mainly European) accounting firms in 1979. Led by Dutch accountants Klynveld Kraayenhof and Company and the German firm Deutsche Treuhand-Gesellschaft, a far-flung alliance was formed. Other notable firms joining the new organization were U.S.-based Main Lafrentz, Thomson McLintock of Britain and the Swiss company Fides Revision. The new super-firm took the name Klynveld Main Goerdeler (KMG), recognizing the contribution of Reinhard Goerdeler, chairman at that time of Deutsche Treuhand-Gesellschaft, in engineering the deal. Less than 10 years later, PMI and KMG would combine to form KPMG.

Stumbling out of the gate

The newly merged KPMG got off to somewhat of a rocky start. First, there were the usual challenges that accompany a major transaction such as the PMI-KMG deal. While merger issues distracted the firm, some major clients were allowed to walk away, resulting in a loss of 10 percent of the company's business. KPMG was also obliged to layoff some of its associates in 1990 as redundant departments were consolidated. In the early 1990s, in a scene eerily similar to today's accounting scandals, the accounting industry was rocked by a series of lawsuits stemming from the failure of savings and loan

(S&L) institutions. The suits questioned the reliability of S&L audits performed by KPMG and the other big accounting firms. KPMG's reputation was further tarnished by the high-profile bankruptcy of Orange County, Calif., in 1994. The Orange County failure resulted in a separate string of lawsuits alleging that the firm was negligent in its role as county auditor and thus contributed to the debacle. Though KPMG insisted that it had done nothing wrong, the suit was eventually settled out of court for $75 million in 1998.

Maneuvering for growth

Throughout the 1990s, consulting revenue came to account for an increasing percentage of the business of Big Five firms. Recasting themselves as professional services companies rather than mere accounting firms, KPMG and the others moved aggressively to capture more consulting business, particularly in the then-booming information technology (IT) sector. In addition to building up in-house consulting practices, KPMG also went out and acquired Marrinan & Associates, a banking consultancy, in 1996.

After Price Waterhouse and Coopers & Lybrand announced their intention to merge in 1997, KPMG briefly flirted with the notion of getting bigger itself. In October 1997, after just two weeks of negotiation, KPMG and Ernst & Young announced an agreement of their own to combine the two professional services heavyweights. The deal was not to be, however. Faced with mounting regulatory opposition in the U.S., Europe and Japan, the proposed merger was called off in 1998.

Consultants cut loose

Months before the Enron scandal broke and over a year before the Sarbanes-Oxley Act, KPMG was the first of the major professional services firms to shed its consulting unit. In February 2000, KPMG reorganized its consulting business into a separate operating company and sold a 20 percent stake in it to Cisco Systems for approximately $1 billion. Exactly one year later, KPMG Consulting was spun off entirely as an independent public company. KPMG Consulting's initial public offering was an immediate hit, with shares rising 25 percent at the close of the first day of trading. The stock sale raised $1.9 billion for the new company. In October 2002, KPMG Consulting further distanced itself from its roots by adopting the name BearingPoint.

Feds examine Xerox's books

Though not quite on the same scale as the spectacular disaster that was Andersen, allegations of professional misconduct have dogged the surviving Big Four firms throughout 2002 and 2003. The highest profile headache for KPMG is the ongoing investigation into Xerox's books. In April 2002, the Securities and Exchange Commission (SEC) filed a complaint against KPMG and announced that it had begun a full-scale investigation into its handling of the Xerox audit. In January 2003, a suit was formally filed against the firm and four of its partners, charging KPMG with fraud and alleging that the company ignored warning signs that its former client Xerox had inflated revenue by $3 billion between 1997 and 2000. The SEC further claims that KPMG replaced an auditor on the Xerox account who had raised concerns about the company's accounting methods. Xerox has already paid $10 million to the SEC to settle the suit, but KPMG intends to fight the charges. The SEC is seeking all of KPMG's Xerox fees in damages. The firm's total revenue from Xerox amounts to $26 million from audits and another $56 million from consulting services over the time period in question.

Collapsing tax shelters

KPMG has also been hit with lawsuits stemming from its sale of tax shelter products to wealthy clients. An Internal Revenue Service (IRS) investigation into tax shelter abuse has netted several former KPMG clients, many of whom are now suing KPMG to recoup their losses. As of July 2003, at least 10 lawsuits have been filed against the firm, with more expected in the coming months. KPMG sold the tax shelter product to an estimated 160 clients. In one case, the estate of a deceased Florida man who was a KPMG client is suing the firm. KPMG had designed a strategy of using stock warrants and swaps to artificially create a $27 million capital loss – a practice that the IRS has ruled unallowable. In a damaging development for KPMG, internal company e-mails surfaced in court in June 2003, showing senior KPMG partners expressing concern over "troublesome issues" with regards to the tax shelter strategy.

Brighter days ahead

Not all of KPMG's recent news has been negative, though. The disintegration of Andersen allowed KPMG to pick up several former affiliates of the disgraced firm. In March 2002, KPMG agreed to acquire Andersen's Japanese business; one month later, the firm added the Andersen units in

South Africa and Thailand. In the U.S., KPMG absorbed former Andersen offices in Seattle; Portland, Ore.; Salt Lake City; Boise, Idaho; San Francisco; Los Angeles; Boston; Philadelphia; and Denver. In July 2003, KPMG moved into a new 45,000 square-foot office space in downtown Portland, a move that became necessary when KPMG's old office space could not accomodate the former Andersen workforce. KPMG has also been courting former Andersen clients – ultimately picking up a total of 167 new accounts. The firm has even wooed some significant clients away from rival Big Four firms. In June 2003, KPMG announced that it had been hired by Pulaski Financial Corporation to provide audit services. Pulaski had been a client of Ernst & Young.

GETTING HIRED

The way in

During the academic year, KPMG regularly conducts information sessions and interviews at various college campuses. Interested applicants should consult their career placement office to see if KPMG will be visiting their campus. If not, students may submit resumes online. The company's web site has information about the interview and hiring process. KPMG also has an internship program, which can be a "stepping stone" to a career with the company. Internship positions are paid and available in the summer as well as the winter/spring semester. (The program begins every January and runs for one to three months, depending on the needs of the individual students and offices involved.)

Fit is a KPMG key

Don't expect too many surprises in KPMG's hiring process; it's pretty average for accounting firms. "The initial campus interview was pretty standard," says one source who, though, admits he had to wait awhile to meet with KPMG again. "The second interview was actually 10 months later, with five different people. I met with the partner, senior manager, two managers and a senior. Each person was assigned a topic to cover, to keep it from being five identical interviews. I don't remember any off-the-wall questions." "I interviewed at my university as a senior and had three interviews along with a couple of social gatherings before I received the offer," reports one contact. "I interviewed with senior accountants, managers and partners."

Interviewers like it when you have an idea of where you'd like to go in life. "I met with four levels of employees: partners, managers, supervisors/peers, and one employee slightly junior to the role I was applying for," says one insider. "I remember each of the partners and mangers asked what my goals were and where I saw myself in three to five years." The contact goes on to say that "most seem to be genuinely interested in matching a candidate with the environment and opportunities. The process for the position took three weeks." Lateral hires will face a similar process. "A number of people who would be your colleagues interview you on a very unstructured, somewhat informal basis," says one accountant who was hired away from another firm. "The process is not at all intimidating, and hiring decisions are based purely on need and available pool of applicants to draw from." A burning need for a particular skill set may force KPMG to expand its scope. "When they need people, some applicants are extended offers even though they wouldn't normally make the cut."

OUR SURVEY SAYS

KPMG State

KPMG's boosters say the firm has a relaxed feel. "My experience has been that in general KPMG is one of the 'less stuffy' of the big firms," says one source. "This is a great aspect of the firm. The people are easygoing and good to work with, and getting projects completed is done with the attitude that you will try to have as much fun as possible." But the firm doesn't always stack up well against other Big Fours. "At times, this does mean that the atmosphere is not as professional as it may be with other firms, and when I've worked with professionals from the other big firms such as Ernst & Young and PricewaterhouseCoopers, it seems that they are a minor step above us. Sort of like they're Harvard and we're the well-run but slightly less grand public university."

State U. has other problems, say its insiders. "The firm culture used to be fairly laid-back and congenial, but it is getting more and more cutthroat as the economy sours," observes one contact. "The firm is definitely a follower in many respects. If the other Big Four firms decided to so something, KPMG would do it, too, regardless of how good an idea it is. But they'd be last to do it, and they don't take the lead in anything." KPMG employees are expert fake laughers; one source notices "much laughing at partners' jokes even when they aren't remotely funny." The firm is watching its pennies. "Believe it or not, [someone] in my group submitted her mileage allowance and was called on it by the HR person who used Mapquest to show that she reported 10 more miles than she actually drove," says a contact. Managers can be demanding. "There are managers who are great to work for, from whom you can learn a lot," says one accountant. "But managers who expect you to live and die to put in hours are far more common. Forget having a family, or even pets."

Stuck at the office

The firm expects tough hours. One insider reports that "60-hour weeks are light weeks, and they can easily go up to 90 or more during busy season. There's definite pressure to get billable hours in, and at the same time, pressure to not exceed budgets. The result is working insane hours, and only reporting a fraction of it. Everyone does it, and upper management turns a blind eye." That hardworking insider continues. "I didn't expect to leave at 5:00 every day when I went into tax, but when 10:00 p.m. is leaving early, it's a bit much. Some people stay until 2:00 a.m. during busy season, and they don't get to come in late. The rest of the year, you don't work as late, but still get pressured to work weekends."

KPMG cash

KPMG's salary structure is flat at the lower levels; it takes a couple of years before things pick up. "New hires typically start at the same salary as everyone else, [and] any material differentiation of salaries only occurs once you've been in the firm for a while," says a source. "Your job rating each year is a significant factor, but if you transfer between regions or practices, you can wind up getting ahead of the pack." KPMG's bottom line is also an important factor. "Firm results and profitability are a much larger factor in what bonus you receive than your individual performance," says a source. "Also, when your bonus is given, there is no stated rationale behind it being 10 percent or 20 percent. You just have to go on the stated strengths, weaknesses and overall rating they give you to figure out how to do better in the future."

Benefits that bend

KPMG offers a flexible benefits package that can be customized to meet the needs of each employee. Standard benefits include a choice of medical plans, an optional flexible medical expense account, vision coverage, a choice of dental plans, disability and life insurance, and prescription drug coverage. The company encourages its workers to continue their education. It even offers cash bonuses to employees who pass the certified public accountant or actuarial certification exams – a KPMG employee who passes all the sections of the actuarial exam can make as much as $20,000. Other notable perks include a mortgage assistance program, tax-free transit passes, an adoption expense reimbursement plan, legal advice and services and a confidential counseling service. Thanks to benefits such as discounted child-care, emergency backup dependent care, flexible work arrangements and paid time off for new parents, KPMG was named one of the "100 Best Companies for Working Mothers" by *Working Mother* magazine in 2002 and 2003.

"There are managers who are great to work for, from whom you can learn a lot. But managers who expect you to live and die to put in hours are far more common. Forget having a family, or even pets."

— *KPMG insider*

McGladrey & Pullen LLP

3600 American Blvd. West
Third Floor
Bloomington, MN 55431-1082
Phone: (952) 835-9930
Fax: (952) 921-7702
www.mcgladrey.com

DEPARTMENTS
Accounting
Audit
Consulting
Human Resources
Information Technology
Insurance
International Tax
Sales and Marketing
Tax
Technical
Telecommunications

THE STATS
Chairman, CEO and Managing Partner: William D. (Bill) Travis
Employer Type: Private partnership
Revenue: $580.0 million (FYE 4/03)
No. of Offices: 100+
No. of Employees: 4,000+

KEY COMPETITORS
BDO Seidman
Deloitte & Touche
Grant Thornton

UPPERS
- Long list of benefits

DOWNERS
- McGladrey who?

EMPLOYMENT CONTACT
Human Resources Department
McGladrey & Pullen
3600 American Blvd. West
Third Floor
Bloomington, MN 55431-1082
Fax: (952) 921-7702

THE SCOOP

Auditing the middle market

McGladrey & Pullen provides audit and attest services, as well as certain tax and consulting services, as one of the so-called "second-tier" accounting firms. The company focuses on mid-sized businesses that are owner managed and include industry specializations such as banks, savings institutions, credit unions, and manufacturing firms, with revenues between $5 million and $250 million annually.

Founded in 1926, McGladrey & Pullen also offers business planning, information technology, transfer tax, business tax consulting, and other services through an affiliation with H&R Block subsidiary RSM McGladrey, whose offices provide McGladrey & Pullen with a global presence. McGladrey & Pullen and RSM McGladrey are separate and independent legal entities, and are member firms of RSM International. Through a professional services agreement between the two firms, clients have access to a variety of services from which to choose to meet their needs.

Like many firms, McGladrey & Pullen has seen a decline in its technology consulting revenue, due to the overall recession. However, the company's strongest growth came in its tax consulting business.

Award-winning culture

In April 2003, the Center for Ethical Business Cultures and Minnesota Society of Financial Service Providers named McGladrey & Pullen a finalist in its 2003 Minnesota Business Ethics Awards (MBEA) program. This program recognizes Minnesota businesses that exemplify and promote ethical conduct for the benefit of the workplace, the marketplace, the environment, and the community. The firm was one of five Minnesota businesses honored as a finalist at the annual awards dinner on April 24 in Bloomington, Minn.

For employees, McGladrey & Pullen stresses ongoing education. The firm offers more than 240 educational courses to employees, and has a variety of programs, including the Women's Mentoring, Leadership Development, Partner Development and Business Advisor programs to help its employees develop and grow.

In addition, McGladrey & Pullen says its focus on the middle market means employees will have the opportunity to deal with the key decision makers at their clients' firms, and will permit each employee to take on greater responsibility more quickly than they would at a larger firm.

Taking over

Recently, McGladrey & Pullen has picked up where others left off. Bolt Technology Corp., a maker of geophysical equipment for offshore seismic exploration for oil and gas, including land and marine air guns, announced on March 19, 2003, in a Form 8-K filing with the Securities and Exchange Commission, that it had selected McGladrey & Pullen as its independent auditor, replacing Deloitte & Touche. Additionally, McGladrey & Pullen recently announced that SureBeam Corp., which makes equipment for irradiating food to improve its safety, had hired the firm to complete an audit. SureBeam had fired two auditors, Deloitte (because Deloitte had raised questions about its accounting practices) and KPMG (because SureBeam said KPMG's fees were too high), according to a September 2003 article in *The New York Times*.

GETTING HIRED

Log on for the lists

On McGladrey & Pullen's detailed careers section of its web site, job seekers can search for openings by category, region, specific office and type of assignment (full time, part time, contract, temp). Candidates can then apply online, or they can create a profile that the firm will match up with opportunities. The site also includes a description of the career path that entry-level recruits can expect, as well as the top 10 reasons to work at the firm, which include "training, client service, integrity and benefits." Speaking of benefits, the careers site contains a list (a pretty long one at that) of the firm's employee benefits, which include a 401(k) with matching, flex-time options, a college savings plan, and medical, dental, vision, long-term disability and life insurance.

"Only during busy season - February to April - do we work more than 40 hours a week."

— Moss Adams insider

Moss Adams LLP

1001 Fourth Avenue
31st Floor
Seattle, WA 98154-1199
Phone: (206) 223-1820
Fax: (206) 652-2098
www.mossadams.com

DEPARTMENTS
Assurance Services
Consulting Services (Business Consulting, Business Valuation Services, Information Technology, Litigation Services, Mergers & Acquisitions, Personal Wealth Services, Research Services, Risk Management, Royalty Compliance, and SEC/Corporate Finance Services)
Tax Services

THE STATS
Chairman and CEO: R. (Bob) Bunting*
Employer Type: Private partnership
Revenue: $175.0 million (FYE 12/02)
No. of Employees: 1,100
No. of Offices: 19

* Rick Anderson will take over as Chairman and CEO as of July 1, 2004.

KEY COMPETITORS
BDO Seidman
Deloitte & Touche
Grant Thornton
KPMG
McGladrey & Pullen
PriceWaterhouseCoopers

UPPERS
- Close-knit culture

DOWNERS
- Larger-firm atmosphere – occasional lapses in communication

EMPLOYMENT CONTACT
recruiter@mossadams.com
www.mossadams.com/careers (entry level and experienced hires)

THE SCOOP

Not Big Four, but growing

Living proof that there's life outside of the Big Four, Moss Adams keeps rolling along. The Seattle-based firm provides assurance, consulting and tax services to companies in many industries, including apparel, construction, dealer services, financial institutions, food processing and agriculture, forest products, hospitality, health care, manufacturing and distribution, securities, energy and telecom, not-for-profits and technology. Moss Adams has 1,100 employees and 200 partners in 19 West Coast offices. The firm was founded in 1913 in Seattle and is considered one of the dominant professional services providers in Washington, Oregon and California.

Moss Adams services are divided into three core areas: assurance, tax and consulting. The assurance unit conducts audits of financial statements and makes sure companies comply with regulatory requirements. The tax division at Moss Adams provides advice and prepares tax returns for corporate and individual clients. Moss Adams Advisory Services (MAAS), the consulting division, advises clients in the following key areas: business consulting, litigation services, business valuation services, information technology, mergers and acquisitions, personal wealth services, research services, risk management, royalty compliance, and SEC/corporate finance services. The firm also has two affiliate companies – Moss Adams Capital and Financial Security Group – that provide investment banking and asset management services, respectively. Finally, Moss Adams is a founding member of Moores Rowland International, a network of over 170 companies worldwide that provide advice and services abroad.

Moving south

Recently, Moss Adams has aggressively expanded in California, combining with other successful accounting practices to build its business in the Golden State. Moss Adams has combined with accounting practices in Los Angeles, San Francisco, Stockton, Sacramento, San Diego and Irvine in recent years. According to Moss Adams chairman and CEO Bob Bunting, the firm doesn't plan to stop this expansion anytime soon. "By any measure, we are the largest firm in Washington and Oregon, and our goal is to be the largest middle-market firm in California," Bunting told the *Puget Sound Business Journal* in January 2002.

GETTING HIRED

Get online and make an impression

Moss Adams's web site, www.mossadams.com, has an extensive career section with job postings, an online application system, and a description of benefits and training opportunities. The firm asks those who are applying via on-campus recruiting to also submit a resume online. For entry-level positions, Moss Adams conducts two rounds of interviews, one on campus and one at its offices. Insiders say applicants can expect "one 30-minute campus interview [and] an office interview with three interviewers." You'll have to make an impression on some pretty important people. "I met with three partners, and was interviewed by the person who would have the most day-to-day contact with me," says a tax associate. The interviews themselves "consisted of just conversations to see how well I would fit in," says a source.

Moss Adams' campus recruiting efforts start in the spring each year and target undergraduate juniors (or students who still have one year left of school). In the spring, candidates can attend firm-sponsored career days to learn more about Moss Adams, and public accounting in general. During the summer, the firm also hosts social events for candidates. Come fall, the formal recruiting process begins. Moss Adams recruits at many of the major schools in the West, including the state universities in Washington, Oregon, California, Idaho, Montana, Wyoming and Hawaii.

OUR SURVEY SAYS

Flowing both ways

Insiders say Moss Adams "encourages growth in [your] career" and "both upstream and downstream evaluations help to improve the working culture." The firm's relatively small size makes for a more relaxed culture. "We are a regional firm," says one source. "It is not a large corporation. The partners are very approachable." Managers and partners don't mistreat their employees since "respect for others is one of the firm's core values." But some complain of "an evident lack of downward communication." According to Moss Adams, the firm "stands by its values as defined by Pillar," the symbol for the firm's human resource initiatives. Pillar's an acronym for "Passion for excellence, Integrity, Leading by example, Lifetime learning, A balanced life, and Respect for others."

The firm's compensation package includes medical, dental, life insurance, disability, dependent care, a 401(k), health care reimbursement, and profit sharing after two complete years of service. "The health care benefits are not good, and they are expensive," says a contact. But according to Moss Adams, the firm "pays 70 percent of the health care benefits for all employees, which results in significant cost savings for employees with families." Moss Adams doesn't have unreasonable expectations when it comes to hours. "Only during busy season – February to April – do we work more than 40 hours a week," says a tax associate. During the busiest times, employees are tapped to work "between 50 and 60 hours a week. During non-busy season, we seldom work more than 40 hours a week."

Lots of training opps

Opinions on training are mixed. "There are many opportunities for training, and there are also many industry experts in different areas that we have available as resources," says one assurance associate. "Training could be better," complains another insider. "We seem to be busy enough that it is hard to fit in training." The firm's Continuing Professional Education (CPE) training sessions are offered for each staff level once a year. Additionally, Moss Adams also offers "niche and specialty training."

Plante & Moran PLLC

27400 Northwestern Highway
Southfield, MI 48034
Phone: (248) 352-2500
Fax: (248) 352-0018
www.plantemoran.com

DEPARTMENTS

Accounting
Consulting
Financial Advisors
Mergers & Acquisitions
Technology

THE STATS

Managing Partner: William M. Hermann
Employer Type: Private company
Revenue: $174.0 million (FYE 6/03)
No of. Employees: 1,300
No. of Offices: 15

KEY COMPETITORS

BDO Seidman
Crowe Chizek
Deloitte & Touche
Ernst & Young
Grant Thornton
KPMG
PricewaterhouseCoopers

UPPERS

- "Culture and co-workers"

DOWNERS

- Regional firm

EMPLOYMENT CONTACT

Human Resources Department
Plante & Moran
27400 Northwestern Highway
Southfield, MI 48034
Phone: (248) 352-2500
Fax: (248) 352-0018
www.plantemoran.com/careers

THE SCOOP

The Great Lake firm

Plante & Moran is rooted firmly in the upper Midwest, with offices located throughout Michigan and Ohio. The company provides accounting and management consulting services to businesses, specializing in construction, real estate, auto dealerships, financial institutions, health services, manufacturing, and service industries, as well as not-for-profit and public sector organizations. Plante & Moran is affiliated with Moores Rowland International, an association of more than 165 independent accounting firms. Plante & Moran also offers accounting and business management solutions to small- and medium-sized businesses through a partnership with AccTrack21 USA. Additionally, Plante & Moran offers opportunities through several entities, including: P&M Corporate Finance, an investment banking/M&A firm; PM Financial Advisors, a firm specializing in individual financial consulting and planning; and PM CRESA, a corporate real estate consulting firm.

Midwestern culture and values

Plante & Moran has tried to provide a variety of outings and events that foster cooperation and comfort among staff, especially as the company's headcount has grown. The company has held cookouts in the parking lot, visits from the Good Humor Truck, scavenger hunts, visits to amusement parks and baseball games, weekend vacations at the beach and even casual dining on the office balcony.

These types of corporate outings led to the firm's fifth consecutive ranking as one of *Fortune* magazine's top employers. In January 2003, *Fortune* ranked Plante & Moran No. 11 on the magazine's annual list of the nation's "Best Companies to Work For," noting a variety of the firm's innovative workplace policies and practices, including its teamwork-based corporate climate, low turnover rate, flexible scheduling, and nontraditional career path options. *Fortune* also noted Plante & Moran's Statement of Principles, which are used to guide business and personal decision making and include ethics, individual freedom, common good, and life balance.

Still, Plante & Moran has time to get down to business. In February 2003, the firm launched the Plante Moran Trust, its own trust bank, using a limited banking charter. The new bank, which has $3 million in capital from Plante

& Moran partners, is approved only for trust activities such as setting up personal trusts, charitable trusts, family foundations, endowments and probate estate administration.

Well-trained firm

Plante & Moran's focus on education isn't just lip service. According to an August 1, 2003, article in the *Partner's Report for CPA Firm Owners*, Plante & Moran identified several areas in which it felt its staff needed to increase its skills, which included technical skills and knowledge, technology tools and applications, general business knowledge, relationship-building skills and judgment. The company then designed its training program to include in-house training, on-the-job learning, book learning and even an intranet designed to allow staff to share knowledge-based data. In order to ensure the program is working, Plante & Moran uses a proprietary performance management system with built-in competency models, and uses a gap-analysis model to ensure that the content in the training fulfills the particular need.

GETTING HIRED

Going big and small

The comprehensive careers section of the Plante & Moran web site (www.plantemoran.com) details the benefits, training and mentoring programs the firm offers its staff; the interview process and how to apply online; the firm's on-campus recruiting schedule; and a job search engine for experienced candidates. For the most part, the firm visits both "large and small" campuses in Michigan and Ohio, including Michigan (both the Ann Arbor and Dearborn campuses), Michigan State, Ohio State, Western Michigan, Eastern Michigan, Albion and Miami of Ohio. On-campus recruits can expect two rounds of interviews. Says one insider, "The on-campus interview is followed by an interview at a preferred office where you'll meet with at least one partner, managers and staff." The contact adds, "Interviews focus on experience, education, skills and outside interests."

OUR SURVEY SAYS

The firm that does unto others...

Insiders say "the golden rule" rules at Plante & Moran. "The culture is the reason I came to Plante & Moran," says one source. "They truly care about each staff member's professional development, and help them maintain a healthy work/life balance." Not only does everyone treat each other well – sources give managers high marks for their treatment of juniors – but "flexibility is promoted, and not frowned-upon." One contact cites "the culture and co-workers" as the two best things about working at the firm.

Training also receives high marks from contacts, as does diversity. "There's a high percentage of female partners and directors," says one contact. Perks include a "401(k) with a 1 percent employer match, 50 percent reimbursement for gym memberships and the option to purchase up to two extra weeks of vacation." As for salary, the firm seems to pay in line with the industry average. One source with less than three years of experience says he'll be getting his first bonus this year because, as he explains, "there's no bonus until you have three full years of experience." Contacts report working anywhere between 40 and 60 hours a week. And don't make weekend plans just yet. Insiders report "frequent" weekend office visits and during tax season, think at least one such visit a week: "You'll work every Saturday from January to April."

PricewaterhouseCoopers LLP

1301 Avenue of the Americas
New York, NY 10019-6022
Phone: (646) 471-4000
Fax: (646) 471-3188
www.pwcglobal.com/us

THE STATS

Chairman and Senior Partner :
Dennis M. Nally
Employer Type: Private partnership (U.S. arm of PricewaterhouseCoopers)
Revenue: $4.7 billion (FYE 6/02)
No. of Employees: 38,000
No. of Offices: 82

KEY COMPETITORS

Deloitte & Touche
Ernst & Young
KPMG

UPPERS

- Big Four reputation
- Premier clients

DOWNERS

- Sometimes rocky culture
- Questions about raises and bonuses

EMPLOYMENT CONTACT

See www.pwcglobal.com/uscareers

THE SCOOP

How do you spell that?

PricewaterhouseCoopers LLP, the U.S. arm of the Big Four accountant PricewaterhouseCoopers, was created in the late 1990s when four of the world's largest accounting firms were considering mergers – Price Waterhouse with Coopers & Lybrand, and KPMG with Ernst & Young. The KPMG/Ernst & Young union failed to materialize, but the Price Waterhouse and Coopers & Lybrand deal went through – creating the capital "P," lower case "w," capital "C," spaceless PricewaterhouseCoopers (PwC) in 1998. The new firm became the largest of the then-Big Five accountancies, with $15 billion in revenue and approximately 140,000 employees (including 10,000 partners), many of whom focus on serving some of the top corporations in the U.S. PwC has an overall market share of Fortune 50, Fortune 100 and Fortune 500 companies of 34 percent, 34 percent and 30 percent, respectively.

By 2002, with the demise of former rival Andersen, the industry was down to a mere Big Four. Also that year, PwC divested itself of its consulting operations, selling the unit to IBM. The consulting business had accounted for nearly 40 percent of the company's revenue. Though today's PwC (the global operation) is markedly smaller following the spin-off, it has retained the top spot among professional services firms. PwC employs over 124,000 people and offers three main lines of business: assurance and business advisory services, tax and legal services, and corporate finance and recovery.

Victorian heritage

Today, many may think of PwC as an American company, but the firm's origins actually lie across the Atlantic Pond. PwC traces its beginnings to 1849 when Samuel Lowell Price opened his accounting practice in London. Five years later, William Cooper opened his own London firm that would soon become known as Cooper Brothers. Price's firm joined with fellow Londoners Holyland and Waterhouse in 1865, and the partnership was renamed Price, Waterhouse & Co. in 1874. In 1957, Cooper merged with the U.S.-based firm Lybrand, Ross Bros., & Montgomery to create Coopers & Lybrand. Price Waterhouse and Coopers & Lybrand were both extremely successful from the 1960s through the 1980s, adding to their slate of services, expanding internationally and bringing automation technology to the audit process. In the early 1990s, though, a wave of consolidation in the professional services industry threatened both firms' ability to compete, necessitating their 1998 merger. Each company brought complementary strengths to the table. While Price Waterhouse's clients had traditionally been centered in the media, entertainment and utility industries, Coopers & Lybrand was known for its expertise in telecommunications and mining.

Long arm of the SEC

PricewaterhouseCoopers was the first casualty of an industry-wide crackdown on the practice of accountants owning stock in companies they audited. The Securities and Exchange Commission (SEC) found in January 2000 that 1,885 PwC employees had ownership stakes in corporations audited by the firm. All told, 8,064 violations were uncovered; 45 percent of those violations were by partners in the firm. While neither admitting nor denying guilt, then-CEO James Schiro and Chairman Nicholas Moore wrote in a letter to the firm's partners that the report was "embarrassing to our firm and to all of us as partners" and that "equally important, it may also raise questions and concerns among our clients."

While the SEC investigation dealt with equity investments, questions about auditor independence have long been a concern at professional services firms. In particular, the firms were sensitive to the appearance of a conflict of interest between the certification of audit work for a client and the substantial revenue the firm might receive for consulting contracts from the same company. Critics suggested that firms might be reluctant to issue critical auditor's reports that could jeopardize a lucrative consulting relationship. The accountants, recognizing the inherent conflicts, began looking for ways to separate their consulting units even before the Andersen/Enron scandal broke in late 2001 and the Sarbanes-Oxley Act went into effect. KPMG spun off its consulting unit in a public offering; Ernst & Young sold its consulting arm to Cap Gemini of France. PwC thought it had struck a similar deal with computer maker Hewlett-Packard in September 2000. That deal fell through two months later, however, when Hewlett-Packard's stock price plummeted, dropping the value of HP's offer from between $17 billion and $18 billion to $15 billion.

PwC's new boss

In July 2001, CEO Schiro announced his intention to step down as soon as a successor was named and a transition could be executed. Though there was speculation that Schiro's departure was related to the failed HP deal (and, to a lesser extent, the SEC auditing probe), the firm and Schiro insisted his departure was amicable. Schiro, who will be best remembered for overseeing the merger between Price Waterhouse and Coopers & Lybrand, was named CEO at Swiss insurer Zurich Financial Services in May 2002.

In November 2001, PwC's board elected Samuel DiPiazza as the new global CEO. DiPiazza joined Coopers & Lybrand in 1973 and served as head of PwC's North American tax services operation and head of PwC's U.S. operations. DiPiazza's reign officially began in early 2002. Dennis Nally, a managing partner of PwC's U.S. business and a 28-year veteran of the firm, succeeded DiPiazza as senior partner of U.S. operations in March 2002.

Big Blue consulting

As PwC continued to wrestle with the future of its consulting arm, the unfolding Andersen/Enron scandal of late 2001 only added to the controversy. Eventually, PwC competitor Arthur Andersen was nailed for its faulty audits of the Houston-based Enron. Critics said that one of the factors at work in Andersen's conviction was the conflict of interest stemming from the firm's consulting work for Enron. The fallout increased pressure on other professional services firms to separate their audit and consulting practices. In January 2002, PwC announced a spin-off of PwC Consulting. The new company soon decided to rename itself Monday, a much-mocked decision that was intended to further emphasize its independence from PricewaterhouseCoopers. Not long after the re-branding announcement, however, PricewaterhouseCoopers had a sudden change of heart. The firm hastily cancelled its spin-off plans and sold PwC Consulting/Monday to IBM instead. The July 2002 deal, worth $3.5 billion, added PwC Consulting to IBM's already formidable consulting operations.

Andersen's loss is PwC's gain

With Arthur Andersen's U.S. operations facing obstruction of justice charges for its role in Enron's bankruptcy, Andersen's innocent overseas affiliates attempted to salvage what they could of a business severely tarnished by their American partners. In March 2002, PwC snapped up a couple of those affiliates, merging with Arthur Andersen's Hong Kong and China units. In all, PwC picked up over 3,500 former Andersen associates; 70 percent of those additions came as a result of the Hong Kong and China acquisitions. According to a PwC spokeswoman, the newly combined Asian operations will have 3,000 employees in Hong Kong and 3,000 more in mainland China.

Silas Yang, the chairman and senior partner of PricewaterhouseCoopers in Hong Kong, praised the "practice and professionalism of our new colleagues," and predicted the combined firm would be a leader in Hong Kong and China.

Additionally, as a result of the Enron scandal, Andersen's clients began dropping the troubled firm as its auditor. PwC was there to pick up the pieces. By early March 2002, even before the criminal indictment against the firm was announced, three of the five largest clients to drop Andersen as its auditor – Merck, Freddie Mac and SunTrust Banks – hired PwC to take over.

Talk's not cheap

In May 2003, PwC agreed to pay $1 million to settle an SEC complaint. The commission had charged the firm with professional misconduct in connection with the audit of SmarTalk TeleServices, a provider of pre-paid phone cards and wireless services that went bankrupt. The SEC complaint alleges that in PwC's 1997 audit of the company, it failed to properly account for a reserve fund of $25 million. As a result, SmarTalk's annual report filed with the SEC that year contained "materially false and misleading financial statements." In addition to the payment, the firm agreed to be censured and pledged to make changes in its procedures. At the time, PwC said, "PricewaterhouseCoopers is glad to put this matter behind us. The agreement pertains to a matter that dates to 1998. We are fully complying with all provisions of the agreement with the SEC." The settlement came less than one year after the firm agreed to pay $5 million to settle other matters with the SEC. That agreement, reached in July 2002, concerned investment banking services provided to 16 public companies between 1996 and 2001. Reacting to these and other incidents in which it has received bad press, PwC began an aggressive ad campaign called "stand and be counted," which, according to the firm, "takes a leading a role in helping to develop solutions to the disclosure and governance issues now front and center on the public agenda."

New partners, new businesses

Courtroom troubles aside, PwC announced some good news in July 2003 – the addition of 288 new partners worldwide and the creation of a new IT Business Risk Management practice. The admission of new partners, including 73 in the United States, brings PwC's worldwide total to approximately 8,000. The new partners come from all of the firm's business units, with the largest contingent in the assurance and business advisory department. Meanwhile, PwC's new IT Business Risk group will work with clients to maximize returns on IT investment and ensure that IT operations are coordinated with current and future business objectives.

And the Oscar goes to?

Not PricewaterhouseCoopers, though the firm does know before anyone else who will win the shiny little men. Since 1935, Price Waterhouse, and then later PricewaterhouseCoopers, has tallied the votes cast by the members of the Academy of Motion Picture Arts and Sciences, which annually doles out the coveted Oscar statues to honor film's best performances. In 2003, PwC partner and eight-year veteran ballot counter Greg Garrison, along with second-time counter and fellow PwC partner Rick Rosas, oversaw the tallying. Before envelopes were opened and teary "thank yous" acted out, Garrison and Rosas were the only two people who knew which stars would take home the hardware.

On Oscar night 2003, as is done each year, the PwC partners each carried briefcases with the golden envelopes and were driven to the show in separate cars under armed guard. Aside from counting votes, Garrison and Rosas also proofed the nominations announcement press release to confirm that the list of nominees was in order. Additionally, PwC representatives must make sure that ballots arrive safely at the post office from Academy headquarters. Apparently, that's not as easy as it sounds. In 2000, ballots for California members of the Academy were lost in the mail. As a result, the Academy was forced to send out new ballots and extend the voting deadline. Eventually, the missing ballots did turn up – at a postal center in a Los Angeles suburb, where they had been accidentally mixed in with bulk mail shipments.

GETTING HIRED

Award-winning recruiting

PricewaterhouseCoopers knows its way around the top campuses. The firm was named the top recruiter among accounting firms two years in a row by the Emerson Company, an accounting industry analyst. Additionally, in a recent survey of accounting faculty in the *Public Accounting Report*, PwC was rated the No. 1 firm among all public accounting firms. The firm has also been recognized for its award-winning recruiting web site, www.pwc.com/lookhere. The firm's "recruiting is focused at PwC 'key schools,'" says one insider. "Therefore, students at other colleges face an additional challenge – but if they are polite and research the correct person to contact, they can get hired." But of course, that doesn't mean stiffs from even the best schools have a free pass at PricewaterhouseCoopers. "I believe they look for personality over grades and schools," says one contact. "They won't hire someone if they don't feel they can work well with a team."

The firm's hiring process is typical of the industry. "I went through the hiring process on campus," says one tax associate. "I interviewed with the recruiter on campus and then was selected for an office visit. They flew me to Pittsburgh at my convenience and I spent the first half of the day in a series of interviews with various managers and finally a partner. I was asked all of the standard questions like tell me a time you worked on a team project and how it worked out, what was your role in the project, how did you handle the other members. Then I was sent to lunch with two associates and when we came back from lunch I was given a job offer."

Some interviewers will try to make you feel welcome. "I was interviewed with the person who showed up at the campus career fair," reports one source. "She asked me my education and family background. She made me feel very comfortable by explaining her education and job background in the beginning of the interview. The specific questions were of my research ability, such as writing a proposal, and my communication skills with other people." The contact adds, "She asked me whether I like to present certain research topics in the office, and my final goal in the job." Some interviewers treat the candidate like a suspect. "The worst interview was when I walked into a conference room and was met by six individuals who tag-teamed me nonstop with technical, personal and sports questions for four hours before breaking for lunch – to which I wasn't invited," recalls one scarred-for-life associate. "After lunch another two-hour Q&A session ensued."

OUR SURVEY SAYS

A culture with some critics

Opinions on PricewaterhouseCooper's culture vary greatly, but those who are unhappy are vocally so. One insider calls the firm a "very professional" company where "quality is number one." Another happy employee says the company is "very open and development oriented. Right from the start you can have quality contact with partners and specialists in the firm. Work/life balance is good provided you keep on top of the work and intensive training. Staff [members] appear laid-back but are very confident, aggressive at times and can be perceived as elitist." Another source raves, "The corporate culture is great. I enjoy everyone I work with."

But when it rains criticisms at PwC, it pours. "PricewaterhouseCoopers is a joke," fumes one source. "They spend more time making sure that we all understand what business casual means than how they treat their employees. Public accounting is a grueling line of work, but it could be made so much less stressful if they spent a little time cultivating a positive work environment." There are other complainers. "This is a company that does not care about its employees," states one enraged staffer. "I should've believed my friends when they said that PwC will use you for 80-hour workweeks as long as they need you."

Your personal satisfaction may vary. "If you are a career-minded, type-A personality, PwC is for you," says one contact. "If you are interested in family life and balance, stay away. Don't get me wrong, working here comes with amazing opportunities to work with brilliant people and to learn a lot, but there are definitely sacrifices that must be considered."

Raises for no one

Compensation issues are another sticking point. Things are fine at the start, then it all goes south. "They offer a competitive starting salary but then you get very little in the way of raises – you are usually about six months behind what they pay the new hires – until you are promoted, and you never get a bonus," gripes a junior employee. The misery lasts for several years. "After being with the firm for two and a half years, I am making what a freshly graduated new hire makes," complains one source. "As raises are only given in September, new hires actually will make $1,000 more than those of us who have been with the firm from the time they are hired in May until raises [in September]. Then we will all make the same." The contact adds," They do give a lot of time off, but that's a joke because you'll have to make up all of the hours that you are out of the office and typically will not ever really be able to utilize the vacation time that they give you."

Bookworms

"Training is pretty decent, although it is intense," says one contact. "We go to training usually once a year for a week and you work your butt off. We even have homework." According to PwC, the firm invests more than $100 million in training, offering over 750 courses for ongoing learning and providing over 800,000 hours in training per year. PwC routinely places among *Working Mother* magazine's top companies for working mothers; employees agree with the publication's assessment of the firm's culture, saying that when female employees encounter problems they're usually endemic to the accounting and professional services industry as a whole. "PwC does a great job hiring women, but the field is not conducive to keeping them for long-term careers, and in more senior positions the numbers drop off dramatically," observes one source. The firm does, though, address these issues: PwC has a dedicated chief diversity officer who has a seat on the firm's U.S. management committee.

THE BEST OF THE REST

Berdon LLP

360 Madison Avenue
New York, NY 10017
Tel. (212) 832-0400
Fax. (212) 371-1159
www.berdonllp.com

DEPARTMENTS

Advertising
Architecture/Engineering Firms
Bankruptcy and Insolvency
Berdon Healthcare Consulting
Corporate Finance
Disaster Preparedness
Entertainment
Estate Planning
Family/Owner-Managed Businesses
Growing Business
Independent Internal Auditing
Law Firm
Litigation & Business Valuation
Nonprofit
Personal Wealth Management,
Personal Business Management,
Financial Consulting
Personal Wealth Management for Attorneys
Real Estate
Real Estate Institutional Investors

THE STATS

Managing Partner: Stanley Freundlich
Employer Type: Private partnership
Revenue: $60.3 million (FYE 12/02)
No. of Employees: 350+
No. of Offices: 2

EMPLOYMENT CONTACT

Melanie Villaruel
Human Resources Administrator
Berdon LLP
360 Madison Avenue
New York, NY 10017
E-mail: mvillaruel@berdonllp.com

Cherry, Bekaert & Holland LLC

1700 Bayberry Court
Suite 300
Richmond, VA 23226-3791
Phone: (804) 673-4224
Fax: (804) 673-4290
www.cbh.com

DEPARTMENTS

Accounting and Auditing Services
Business Valuation Services
Corporate Income Tax
Cost Segregation Studies
Services to Financial Institutions
Government Contract Consulting
Information Systems Consulting
Mergers and Acquisitions
Personal Income Tax
Strategic Management Services
Technology and
Telecommunications

THE STATS

Managing Partner: Howard Kies
Employer Type: Private company
Revenue: $54.8 million (FYE 4/03)
No. of Employees: 500
No. of Offices: 17

EMPLOYMENT CONTACT

College Recruiting
Cherry, Bekaert & Holland, L.L.P.
ATTN: Recruiting Manager
1700 Bayberry Court, Suite 300
Richmond, VA 23226-3791
Fax: (804) 673-5799, ATTN: Recruiting Manager
E-mail: recruiting@cbh.com

Experienced professionals
www.cbh.com/careers.home.htm

Dixon Odom PLLC

1829 Eastchester Dr.
High Point, NC 27261-2612
Phone: (336) 889-5156
www.dixonodom.com

DEPARTMENTS

Assurance
Business Valuation and Litigation
Fraud & Forensic
Corporate Governance
EDP & Internet Assurance
Family Business
PROFIT
Information Technology
Management Advisory Services (MAS)
Corporate Finance
Organizational Development
Human Capital Management
Software Solutions
Tax

THE STATS

Executive Partner: Eddie Sams
Employer Type: Private partnership
Revenue: $57.0 million (FYE 5/03)
No. of Employees: 450+
No. of Offices: 17

EMPLOYMENT CONTACT

Kim Bullard
Phone: (919) 776-0555
E-mail: kbullard@dixonodom.com
www.dixonodom.com/careers.htm

Eide Bailly LLP

406 Main Avenue, Suite 300
P.O. Box 2545
Fargo, ND 58108-2545
Phone: (701) 239-8500
Fax: (701) 239-8600
www.eidebailly.com

DEPARTMENTS

Accounting Services
Audit Services
Business Brokerage
Business Consulting
Business Valuation
Corporate Finance
Employee Benefit Plan Compliance
Farm Accounting & Tax
Medical Practice Management
Peer Review Services
SEC Services
Tax Services
Wealth Transfer Services

THE STATS

CEO: Jerry Topp
Employer Type: Private partnership
Revenue: $62.1 million (FYE 4/03)
No. of Employees: 652
No. of Offices: 10

EMPLOYMENT CONTACT

Brandie Berg: bberg@eidebailly.com

Eisner LLP

750 Third Avenue
New York, NY 10017
Phone: (212) 949-8700
Fax: (212) 891-4100
www.eisnerllp.com

DEPARTMENTS

Audit and Accounting
Corporate Tax Planning
Individual and Family Tax Planning
Corporate Finance
Legal Support Services
Personal Financial Services
Small Business Services
Employee and Executive Benefits
Human Resource Strategies
Corporate Restructuring
Bankruptcy and Insolvency Services
E-Commerce
Information Technology Consulting
Software Selection and Implementation
Operations Management
Data and Telecommunications Networks

THE STATS

CEO and Managing Partner: Richard Eisner
Employer Type: Private partnership
Revenue: $69.0 million (FYE 1/03)
No. of Employees: 400 (approx.)
No. of Offices: 3

EMPLOYMENT CONTACT

www.eisnerllp.com/careers/careers.cfm

Goodman & Co.

One Commercial Place
Norfolk, VA 23510-2119
Phone: (757) 624-5100
Fax: (757) 624-5233
www.goodmanco.com

DEPARTMENTS

Accounting
Auditing and Accounting
Business Valuation
Employee Benefit Services
Estate Planning
Financial Planning
Management Consulting
Tax Credits and Financial Incentives
Tax Planning and Preparation Consulting
Business Planning
Government Contract Consulting
Human Resource Management
Organization & Operational Reviews
Profit Enhancement
Strategic Planning

THE STATS

Managing Partner: Pat Viola
Employer Type: Private company
Revenue: $43.2 million (FYE 6/03)
No. of Employees: 450
No. of Offices: 11

EMPLOYMENT CONTACT

www.goodmanco.com/goodco/careers.asp

J.H. Cohn LLP

75 Eisenhower Parkway
Roseland, NJ 07068
Phone: (973) 228-3500
Fax: (973) 228-0330
www.jhcohn.com

DEPARTMENTS

Accounting and Auditing
Benefits Consulting
Business Investigation Services
Cost Segregation Studies
Estate Planning
Executive Search
Financing Services
Internal Audit Services
International Business
Management Consulting
Mergers and Acquisitions
Networking and Software Solutions
Special Outsource Services
Tax Services
Wealth Management

THE STATS

CEO: Thomas J. Marino
Employer Type: Private partnership
Revenue: $70.3 million (FYE 1/03)
No. of Employees: 600+
No. of Offices: 10

EMPLOYMENT CONTACT

Stanley Stempler
Director of Human Resources
Phone: (973) 228-3500
E-mail: sstempler@jhcohn.com.
www.jhcohn.com/careers/careers.cfm

LarsonAllen (Larson, Allen, Weishair & Co. LLP)

220 South Sixth Street
Suite 300
Minneapolis, MN 55402-1436
Phone: (612) 376-4500
Fax: (612) 376-4850
www.larsonallen.com

DEPARTMENTS

Assurance/Accounting
Executive Search
Information Security
Litigation/Valuation
Tax Services

THE STATS

CEO: Gordon A. Viere
Employer Type: Private partnership
Revenue: $83.8 million (FYE 10/02)
No. of Employees: 750
No. of Offices: 8

EMPLOYMENT CONTACT

www.larsonallen.com/aboutus/hr_main.asp

Parente Randolph LLC

Two Penn Center Plaza
Suite 1800
Philadelphia PA 19102-1725
Phone: (215) 972.0701
Fax: (215) 563.4925
www.parentenet.com

DEPARTMENTS

Assurance Services
Business Reorganization
Corporate Finance
Energy Consulting
Forensic Accounting &
Fundraising Consulting
HR Services
Litigation Services
Management Consulting
Retirement & Estate Planning
Tax Services
Technology

THE STATS

CEO: Robert Ciaruffoli
Employer Type: Private partnership
Revenue: $44.9 million (FYE 10/02)
No. of Employees: 350+
No. of Offices: 18

EMPLOYMENT CONTACT

www.parentenet.com/careers.htm

Reznick Fedder & Silverman

7700 Old Georgetown Road
Suite 400
Bethesda, MD 20814-6224
Phone: (301) 652-9100
Fax: (301) 652-1848
www.rfs.com

DEPARTMENTS

Audit & Accounting
Government Services Group
Internal Audit
Lenders & Investors
Litigation Support Services
Management Consulting
Outsourced Financial Accounting Services
State & Local Tax
Tax Consulting
Valuation

THE STATS

Managing Partners: David Reznick, Stuart Fedder and Ivan Silverman
Employer Type: Private partnership
Revenue: $64.7 million (FYE 9/02)
No. of Employees: 600
No. of Offices: 5

EMPLOYMENT CONTACT

www.rfs.com/careers.shtml

Rothstein, Kass & Co.

85 Livingston Avenue
Roseland, NJ 07068
Phone: (973) 994-6666
Fax: (973) 994-0337
www.rkco.com

DEPARTMENTS

Accounting and Auditing
Coaching and Affiliation
Due Diligence
Litigation Support/Forensic
  Accounting
Management Advisory Services
Mergers and Acquisitions
Personal Financial Planning
Tax Planning and Compliance
SEC Services

THE STATS

Managing Principal: Harris Rothstein
Employer Type: Private
Revenue: $58.0 million company (FYE 12/02)
No. of Employees: 510
No. of Offices: 8

EMPLOYMENT CONTACT

New York/New Jersey
Attn: Human Resources – WS
85 Livingston Avenue
Roseland, NJ 07068
Fax: (973) 994-0337
E-mail: hr-east@rkco.com

Beverly Hills/San Francisco/Dallas
Attn: Human Resources – WS
9171 Wilshire Boulevard, Suite 500
Beverly Hills, CA 90210
Fax: (310) 273-6649
E-mail: hr-west@rkco.com

Schenk Business Solutions

200 E. Washington Street
P.O. Box 1739
Appleton, WI 54912-1739
Phone: (920) 731-8111;
(800) 236-2246
Fax: (920) 731-8037
www.schencksolutions.com

DEPARTMENTS

Accounting & Auditing
Business Consulting
Estate & Trust Planning
HR Consulting
International Business Solutions
Investment Management
Mergers & Acquisitions
Payroll Services
Retirement Plan Administration
Tax Planning & Compliance
Technology Solutions
Valuations & Litigation

THE STATS

President: William D. Goodman
Employer Type: Private company
Revenue: $49.4 million (FYE 10/02)
No. of Employees: 600+
No. of Offices: 13

EMPLOYMENT CONTACT

www.schencksolutions.com/careers.htm

Virchow, Krause & Co.

10 Terrace Court
Madison, WI 53718
Phone: (608) 249-6622
www.virchowkrause.com

DEPARTMENTS

Accounting & Assurance
Business Advisory
Business Process Improvement
Employee Benefits
Energy Market
Insurance
Investment Management
Mergers and Acquisitions
Staffing
Tax
Technology
Wealth Management

THE STATS

CEO: Tim Christen
Employer Type: Private partnership
Revenue: $104.1 million (FYE 5/03)
No. of Employees: 850+
No. of Offices: 12

EMPLOYMENT CONTACT

careers.virchowkrause.com

Weiser LLP

135 West 50th Street
New York, NY 10020
Phone: (212).812-7000
Fax: (212).375-6888
www.weiserllp.com

DEPARTMENTS

Auditing and Accounting
Business Consulting
Business Investigation Services
Corporate Finance
Executive Search
IT Consulting
Insurance
International Services
Investment Advisory Services
Litigation Support
Outsourcing Management
Pension, Benefits, and Compensation
Personal Financial Planning
Private Client Services
Royalty Compliance Services
SEC Services
Tax Planning and Compliance
Trusts and Estates
Turnaround and Bankruptcy

THE STATS

Managing Partner: Andy Cohen
Employer Type: Private partnership
Revenue: $53.0 million (FYE 12/02)
No. of Employees: 280
No. of Offices: 3

EMPLOYMENT CONTACT

John Porricelli
Director of Human Resources
Weiser LLP
135 West 50th Street
New York, NY 10020
E-mail: jporricelli@mrweiser.com

Wipfli (Wipfli Ullrich Bertelson LLP)

11 Scott Street
Wausau, WI 54403
Phone: (715) 845-3111
Fax: (715) 842-7272
www.wipfli.com

EMPLOYMENT CONTACT

www.wipfli.com/career_choices/Overview.asp

DEPARTMENTS

Information Technology and Business Improvement Services
Accounting Systems Implementation and Support
Business Process Improvement
Electronic Commerce and Groupware Solutions
Executive Information and Decision Support Systems
Information Systems Planning, Design, and Implementation

Financial Planning and Tax Services
Retirement and Estate Planning
Administration and Consulting
Employee Benefit Plan
Personal Financial Planning
Tax Planning and Strategies

Management/Business Consulting
Accounting, Auditing, and Tax
Business Valuation Services
Family Business Services
Human Resource Consulting
Marketing Consulting
Strategic Business Planning

THE STATS

Managing Partner: Greg Barber
Employer Type: Private partnership
Revenue: $59.0 million (FYE 5/03)
No. of Employees: 600+
No. of Offices: 17

APPENDIX

Decrease your T/NJ Ratio
(Time to New Job)

Use the Internet's most targeted job search tools for finance professionals.

Vault Finance Job Board

The most comprehensive and convenient job board for finance professionals. Target your search by area of finance, function, and experience level, and find the job openings that you want. No surfing required.

VaultMatch Resume Database

Vault takes match-making to the next level: post your resume and customize your search by area of finance, experience and more. We'll match job listings with your interests and criteria and e-mail them directly to your inbox.

VAULT
> the most trusted name in career information™

Glossary

Accelerated depreciation: Any depreciation method that writes off depreciable costs more quickly than the ordinary straight-line method.

Account payable: A liability that results from a purchase of goods or services on open account.

Accounting: The process of identifying, recording, summarizing and reporting economic information to decision makers.

Accounting controls: The methods and procedures for authorizing transactions, safeguarding assets and ensuring the accuracy of financial controls.

Accounting Principles Board (APB): The predecessor of the Financial Accounting Standards Board (FASB).

Accounting system: A set of records, procedures and equipment that routinely deals with the events affecting the financial performance and position of the entity.

Account receivable: An amount owed to a company by customers as a result of delivering goods or services and extending credit in the ordinary course of business.

Accrual basis: Accounting method that recognizes the impact of transactions on the financial statements in the time periods when revenues and expenses occur.

Accrue: To accumulate a receivable or payable during a given period even though no explicit transaction occurs.

Accumulated depreciation: The cumulative sum of all depreciation recognized since the date of acquisition of the particular assets described.

Administrative controls: All methods and procedures that facilitate management planning and control of operations.

American Institute of Certified Public Accountants (AICPA): The leading organization of the auditors of corporate financial reports.

Allowance for doubtful accounts: A contra asset account that measures the amount of receivables estimated to be uncollected.

Amortization: When referring to long-lived assets, it usually means the allocation of the costs of intangible assets to the periods that benefit from these assets.

Annual report: A combination of financial statements, management discussion and analysis, and graphs and charts that is provided annually to investors.

APB Opinions: A series of 31 opinions of the Accounting Principles Board, many of which are still in effect.

Assets: Economic resources that are expected to benefit future cash inflows or help reduce future cash outflows.

Audit: An examination of transactions and financial statements made in accordance with generally accepted auditing standards.

Audit committee: A committee of the board of directors that oversees the internal accounting controls, financial statements and financial affairs of the corporation.

Auditor: A person that examines the information used by managers to prepare the financial statements and attests to the credibility of those statements.

Auditor's opinion: A report describing the auditor's examination of transactions and financial statements, included with the financial statements in an annual report issued by the corporation.

Bad debt expense: The cost of granting credit that arises from uncollectible accounts.

Balance sheet (statement of financial condition): A financial statement that shows the financial status of a business entity at a particular moment in time.

Balance sheet equation: Assets = Liabilities + Owners' Equity.

Book value (carrying value): The balance of an account shown on the books, net of any contra accounts.

Capital: A term used to identify owners' equities for proprietorships and partnerships.

Capitalization (capital structure): Owners' equity plus long-term debt.

Capitalized: A cost that is added to an asset account, as distinguished from being expensed immediately.

Cash basis: Accounting method that recognizes the impact of transactions on the financial statements only when cash is received or disbursed.

Cash equivalents: Highly liquid short-term investments that can easily be converted to cash.

Cash flows from financing activities: The third major section of the statement of cash flows, describing flows to and from providers of capital.

Cash flows from investing activities: The second major section of the statement of cash flows, describing the purchases and sales of plant, property, equipment and other long-lived assets.

Cash flows from operating activities: The first major section of the statement of cash flows, showing the cash effects of transactions that affect the income statement.

Certified public accountant (CPA): In the United States, a person earns this designation by a combination of education, qualifying experience and the passing of a written examination.

Common stock: Stock representing the class of owners having a "residual" ownership of a corporation.

Conservatism: Selecting accounting methods and treatments that yield lower net income, lower assets, and/or lower stockholders' equity.

Consolidated statements: Combinations of the financial positions and earnings of the parent company with those of various subsidiaries into an overall report as if they were a single entity.

Contingent liability: A potential liability, often off-balance sheet, which depends on the occurrence of a future event arising out of a past transaction.

Contra account: A separate but related account that offsets or is a deduction from a companion account.

Cost of goods available for sale: Sum of beginning inventory and current year purchases.

Cost of goods sold (cost of sales): The original acquisition cost of the inventory that was sold to customers during the reporting period.

Cost recovery: The concept by which some purchases of goods or services are recorded as assets because their costs are expected to be recovered in the form of cash inflows, or reduced cash outflows, in future periods.

Credit: An entry or balance on the right side of an account.

Current assets: Cash plus assets that are expected to be converted to cash, sold or consumed during the next 12 months (or within the normal operating cycle if longer than a year).

Current liabilities: Liabilities that fall due within the coming year (or within the normal operating cycle if longer than a year).

Current ratio (working capital ratio): Current assets divided by current liabilities.

Debit: An entry or balance on the left side of an account.

Debt-to-equity ratio: Total liabilities divided by total shareholders' equity.

Depletion: The process of allocating the cost of natural resources to the periods in which the resources are used.

Depreciable value: The amount of the acquisition cost to be allocated as depreciation over the total useful life of an asset. It is the difference between the total acquisition cost and the predicted residual value.

Depreciation: The allocation of the acquisition cost of long-lived or fixed assets to the expense accounts of particular periods that benefit from the use of the assets.

Dilution: Reduction in stockholders' equity per share or earnings per share that arises from changes among shareholders' proportional interests.

Discontinued operations: The termination of a business segment, the results of which are reported separately, net of tax, in the income statement.

Dividend-payout ratio: Common dividends per share divided by earnings per share.

Dividend-yield ratio: Common dividends per share divided by market price per share.

Double-declining-balance depreciation (DDB): The most popular form of accelerated depreciation, computed by doubling the straight-line rate and multiplying the resulting DDB rate by the beginning book value.

Double-entry system: The method usually followed for recording transactions, whereby at least two accounts are always affected by each transaction.

Earnings per share (EPS): Net income divided by average number of common shares outstanding.

EBIT: Earnings before interest and taxes.

EBITDA: Earnings before interest, taxes, depreciation and amortization.

Expenses: Decreases in owners' equity that arise because goods or services are delivered to customers.

Extraordinary items: Items that are unusual in nature and infrequent in occurrence that are shown separately, net of tax, in the income statement.

Financial accounting: The field of accounting that serves external decision makers, such as stockholders, suppliers, banks and government agencies.

Financial Accounting Standards Board (FASB): A private-sector body that determines generally accepted accounting principles in the United States.

Financing activities: Activities that involve obtaining resources as a borrower or issuer of securities and repaying creditors and owners.

First-in, first-out (FIFO): A method of inventory accounting that assigns the cost of the earliest acquired units to cost of goods sold first.

Fiscal year: The year established for accounting purposes.

General ledger: The collection accounts that accumulates the amounts reported in the major financial statements.

Generally Accepted Accounting Principles (GAAP): A term that applies to the broad concepts or guidelines and detailed practices in accounting, including all the conventions, rules and procedures that make up accepted accounting practice.

Goodwill: The excess of the cost of an acquired company over the sum of the fair market value of its identifiable individual assets less the liabilities.

Gross profit (gross margin): The excess of sales revenue over the cost of the inventory that was sold.

Gross sales: Total sales revenue before deducting sales returns and allowances.

Historical cost: The amount originally paid to acquire an asset.

Income statement (statement of earnings): A report of all revenues and expenses pertaining to a specific time period.

Intangible assets: Rights or economic benefits, such as patents, trademarks, copyrights and goodwill, that are not physical in nature.

Internal control: System of checks and balances that assures that all actions occurring within the company are in accordance with organizational objectives.

Inventory: Goods held by a company for the purpose of sale to customers.

Investing activities: Activities that involve (1) providing and collecting cash as a lender or as an owner of securities and (2) acquiring and disposing of plant, property, equipment and other long-term productive assets.

Journal entry: An analysis of the effects of a transaction on the accounts, usually accompanied by an explanation.

Last-in, first-out (LIFO): An inventory method that assigns most recent costs to cost of goods sold.

Ledger: The records for a group of related accounts kept current in a systematic manner.

Liabilities: Economic obligations of the organization to outsiders or claims against its assets by outsiders.

Long-lived assets: Resources held for an extended time, such as land, buildings, equipment, natural resources and patents.

Long-term liabilities: Obligations that fall due beyond one year from the balance sheet date.

Lower-of-cost-or-market method (LCM): The superimposition of a market-price test on an inventory cost method.

Management accounting: The field of accounting that serves internal decision makers, such as top executives, department heads, administrators and people at other levels of management within an organization.

Management's discussion and analysis (MD&A): A required section of annual reports that concentrates on explaining the major changes in the income statement, liquidity and capital resources.

Matching: The recording of expenses in the same time period as the related revenues that are recognized.

Materiality convention: The concept that a financial statement item is material if its omission or misstatement would tend to mislead the reader of the financial statements.

Net income: The remainder after all expenses have been deducted from revenues.

Net sales: Total sales revenue reduced by sales returns and allowances.

Notes payable: Promissory notes that are evidence of a debt and state the payment terms.

Operating activities: Transactions that affect the income statement.

Operating income: Gross profit less all operating expenses.

Outstanding shares: Shares remaining in the hands of shareholders.

Owners' equity: The residual interest in the organization's assets after deducting liabilities.

Paid-in capital: The total capital investment in a corporation by its owners at the inception of the business and subsequently.

Par value: The nominal dollar amount printed on stock certificates.

Permanent differences: Revenue or expense items that are recognized for tax purposes but not recognized for GAAP, or vice versa.

Pretax income: Income before income taxes.

Price-earnings ratio (P-E): Market price per share of common stock divided by earnings per share of common stock.

Private accountants: Accountants who work for businesses, government agencies and other nonprofit organizations.

Public accountants: Accountants who offer services to the general public on a fee basis including auditing, tax work and management consulting.

Recognition: A test for determining whether revenues should be recorded in the financial statement of a given period. To be recognized, revenues must be earned and realized.

Reserve: Has one of three meanings: (1) a restriction of dividend-declaring power as denoted by a specific subdivision of retained income, (2) an offset to an asset, or (3) an estimate of a definite liability of indefinite or uncertain amount.

Residual value (terminal value, salvage value): The amount received from disposal of a long-lived asset at the end of its useful life.

Retained income (retained earnings): Additional owners' equity generated by income.

Revenues (sales): Increases in owners' equity arising from increases in assets received in exchange for the delivery of goods or services to customers.

Special items: Expenses that are large enough and unusual enough to warrant separate disclosure.

Statement of cash flows: A statement that reports the cash receipts and cash payments of an entity during a particular period.

Stockholders' equity (shareholders' equity): Owners' equity of a corporation. The excess of assets over liabilities.

Straight-line depreciation: A method that spreads the depreciable value evenly over the useful life of an asset.

T-account: Simplified version of ledger accounts.

Tangible assets (fixed assets): Physical items that can be seen and touched.

Timing differences (temporary differences): Differences between net income and taxable income that arise because some revenue and expense items are recognized at different times for tax purposes than for reporting purposes.

Treasury stock: A corporation's issued stock that has subsequently been repurchased by the company and not retired.

Trial balance: A list of all accounts in the general ledger with their balances.

Uncollectible accounts (bad debts): Receivables determined to be uncollectible because debtors are unable or unwilling to pay their debts.

Unearned revenue (deferred revenue): Revenue received and recorded before it is earned.

Useful life: The time period over which an asset is depreciated.

Working capital: The excess of current assets over current liabilities.

Write-down: A reduction in the assumed cost of an item in response to a decline in value.

Competition on the Street – and beyond – is heating up. With the finance job market tightening, you need to be your best.

We know the finance industry. And we've got experts that know the finance environment standing by to review your resume and give you the boost you need to snare the financial position you deserve.

Finance Resume Writing and Resume Reviews

- Have your resume reviewed by a practicing finance professional.
- For resume writing, start with an e-mailed history and 1- to 2-hour phone discussion. Our experts will write a first draft, and deliver a final draft after feedback and discussion.
- For resume reviews, get an in-depth, detailed critique and rewrite within TWO BUSINESS DAYS.

Finance Career Coaching

Have a pressing finance career situation you need Vault's expert advice with? We've got experts who can help.

- Trying to get into investment banking from business school or other careers?
- Switching from one finance sector to another – for example, from commercial banking to investment banking?
- Trying to figure out the cultural fit of the finance firm you should work for?

"Thank you, thank you, thank you! I would have never come up with these changes on my own!"
– W.B., Associate, Investment Banking, NY

"Having an experienced pair of eyes looking at the resume made more of a difference than I thought."
– R.T., Managing Director, SF

"I found the coaching so helpful I made three appointments!"
– S.B., Financial Planner, NY

For more information go to http://finance.vault.com

VAULT
> the most trusted name in career information™

About the Author

Derek Loosvelt is a graduate of the Wharton School at the University of Pennsylvania. He is a writer and editor and has worked for *Brill's Content*, Inside.com and *blue* magazine. Previously, he worked in investment banking at CIBC and Duff & Phelps.

VAULT CAREER GUIDES
GET THE INSIDE SCOOP ON TOP JOBS

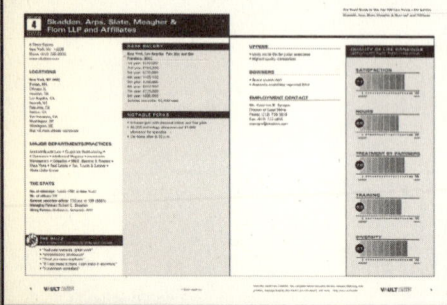

"Cliffs Notes for Careers"
– FORBES MAGAZINE

Vault guides and employer profiles have been published since 1997 and are the premier source of insider information on careers.

Each year, Vault surveys and interviews thousands of employees to give readers the inside scoop on industries and specific employers to help them get the jobs they want.

"To get the un-varnished scoop, check out Vault"
– SMARTMONEY MAGAZINE

VAULT

Get the BUZZ on Top Schools

Read what STUDENTS and ALUMNI have to say about:

- Admissions
- Academics
- Career Opportunities
- Quality of Life
- Social Life

Surveys on thousands of top programs

College • MBA • Law School • Grad School

VAULT

> the most trusted name in career information™

Go to www.vault.com

Decrease your T/NJ Ratio
(Time to New Job)

Use the Internet's most targeted job search tools for finance professionals.

Vault Finance Job Board

The most comprehensive and convenient job board for finance professionals. Target your search by area of finance, function, and experience level, and find the job openings that you want. No surfing required.

VaultMatch Resume Database

Vault takes match-making to the next level: post your resume and customize your search by area of finance, experience and more. We'll match job listings with your interests and criteria and e-mail them directly to your inbox.

VAULT
> the most trusted name in career information™

Do you have an interview coming up with a financial institution?

Unsure how to handle a finance Interview?

Vault Live Finance Interview Prep

Vault brings you a new service to help you prepare for your finance interviews. Your 1-hour live session with a Vault finance expert will include an actual 30-minute finance interview, which will be immediately followed by a 30-minute critique and Q&A session with your expert.

Investment Banking/Corporate Finance Interview Prep

This session preps you for questions about:

- Mergers & acquisitions
- Valuation models
- Accounting concepts
- Personality fit for investment banking and corporate finance positions
- And more!

Sales & Trading Interview Prep

This session prepares you for questions about:

- Capital markets
- Macroeconomics, including impact of different pieces of economic data on securities prices
- Trading strategies
- Interest rates
- Securities including equities, fixed income, currencies, options, and other derivatives
- Personality fit for sales & trading positions
- And more!

For more information go to http://finance.vault.com

VAULT
> the most trusted name in career information™

VAULT CAREER GUIDES
GET THE INSIDE SCOOP ON TOP JOBS

"Cliffs Notes for Careers"
– *FORBES MAGAZINE*

Vault guides and employer profiles have been published since 1997 and are the premier source of insider information on careers.

Each year, Vault surveys and interviews thousands of employees to give readers the inside scoop on industries and specific employers to help them get the jobs they want.

"To get the un-varnished scoop, check out Vault"
– *SMARTMONEY MAGAZINE*

VAULT

Competition on the Street – and beyond – is heating up. With the finance job market tightening, you need to be your best.

We know the finance industry. And we've got experts that know the finance environment standing by to review your resume and give you the boost you need to snare the financial position you deserve.

Finance Resume Writing and Resume Reviews

- Have your resume reviewed by a practicing finance professional.
- For resume writing, start with an e-mailed history and 1- to 2-hour phone discussion. Our experts will write a first draft, and deliver a final draft after feedback and discussion.
- For resume reviews, get an in-depth, detailed critique and rewrite within TWO BUSINESS DAYS.

Finance Career Coaching

Have a pressing finance career situation you need Vault's expert advice with? We've got experts who can help.

- Trying to get into investment banking from business school or other careers?
- Switching from one finance sector to another – for example, from commercial banking to investment banking?
- Trying to figure out the cultural fit of the finance firm you should work for?

"Thank you, thank you, thank you! I would have never come up with these changes on my own!"
– W.B., Associate, Investment Banking, NY

"Having an experienced pair of eyes looking at the resume made more of a difference than I thought."
– R.T., Managing Director, SF

"I found the coaching so helpful I made three appointments!"
– S.B., Financial Planner, NY

For more information go to http://finance.vault.com

VAULT
> the most trusted name in career information™

Wondering what it's like to work at a specific employer?

Read what EMPLOYEES have to say about:
- Workplace culture
- Compensation
- Hours
- Diversity
- Hiring process

Read employer surveys on THOUSANDS of top employers.

VAULT

> the most trusted name in career information™

Go to www.vault.com